ALAN HEAP

HINDSIGHT IS 2020

Purple Monster | Leamington Spa

© Copyright Alan Heap
with additional material
by Harry Heap 2021

Designed by Craig Spivey

Typeset in Avenir and Perpetua
All images from Adobe Stock unless otherwise stated

Published by Purple Monster

ISBN number 978-1-8384882-0-8

A CIP catalogue record of this book is available from
the British Library

4WORD

When Alan asked me to write this foreword, he very quickly explained that there wouldn't be a fee.

I'm delighted to say it didn't put me off and it's my absolute pleasure to have the opportunity of writing the first words in the book.

I first met Alan and the Purple Monster team when we were engaged in a transformation programme for a large UK utility. It was a complex change project with plenty of hard yards to cover and the *Will It Make The Boat Go Faster?* principles were front and centre of the change effort. Alan and his small team were responsible for 'engagement' and although I wasn't entirely sure what they were up to, they looked to be having more fun than they really should, but were crucially helping others on the project team do the same. I've spent a lifetime studying how critical it is for people to be motivated and have fun whilst striving for tough goals and I liked what I saw. That was more than 12 years ago and our paths have crossed many, many times since then and we've shared platforms around the globe, having fun together.

As well as fun, he and the company thrive on creativity and so it came as no surprise to hear about this poetic endeavour. I can promise, as the title of one poem suggests, a full range of emotions for the reader.

Alan is a great storyteller, and the poems document the story of his and many other peoples' lockdown year.

He shares the weekly episodes with humour and humility in equal measure and has created a unique journal of a year so many of us will never forget.

Ben Hunt-Davis MBE
Olympic Gold Medallist
and co-author of
Will It Make The Boat Go Faster?

CONTENTS

DEAR READER

Thanks for buying this book. The story of 2020 lies within these pages, in 52 easy-to-read poems. Pick a title or a date you like and off you go. If, like me, you read your poetry out loud, well then other people on the bus, train, plane or metro will get to enjoy them with you.

Having completed the poems at the start of 2021, it was brilliant to see poetry leading the way at the US presidential inauguration. President Biden's decision to feature poetry followed three others: Presidents Kennedy, Clinton and Obama, all lovers of language.

I was moved to tears watching Amanda Gorman recite 'The Hill We Climb'. She certainly wouldn't have been invited to perform at the previous ceremony. Powerful stuff, poetry.

I do hope you enjoy mine.

Yours with thanks,
Alan

P.S. Should you so desire, you can hear me read the 52 poems by using the QR code below. Each has its own unique introduction, which I recorded week by week during the year of the pandemic.

Who ordered the poetry performance?

The first poem of the 'promised' 52 and the beginning of 2020. The start of the year arrived without fanfare, but there were hints of what was to come with my references to Brexit and racism. For international readers, Geoffrey Boycott is an outspoken ex England cricket player and Twitter user.

A PROMISING

START

t's done, it's here. Welcome 2020, a promising New Year.
What's to be? What's to do? What's to hope for? What's your new?
Santa's gone, left us Brexit—an exit from Europe
But no one's moved my border or ordered me out, yet.
I do detect an undertone. Racist, nasty, in yer face,
Out of place for me, so I'll not play. I'll say no.
I was racist once. 1970s Bradford teenager, knew no better
No one let us know how life would change at school. Fools. No, change management tools.
I'm older now and know to choose; my own views—mostly, but it still takes practice.
'Mindset' is the modern mantra, for all of us the key
                    To how we think about Boris or Brexit or saving the bee.
                    Dweck changed our thinking, psychological resilience;
                    Brilliance isn't what you're born with—it's how you learn that matters.
I can change the world, why not? I can twitter Geoffrey Boycott.
I can influence, be at my best. 'Community' can do the rest.
But the media world is all consuming, girls v boys, right, left, fuming!
Go Placidly amidst the noise, that's my fragment of choice
As the news blurs past and skews the view,
Keep in focus what's dear to you, near to you:
Family, friends, colleagues, neighbours, do the things you ought to.
Oh, and remember everyone, drink more water.

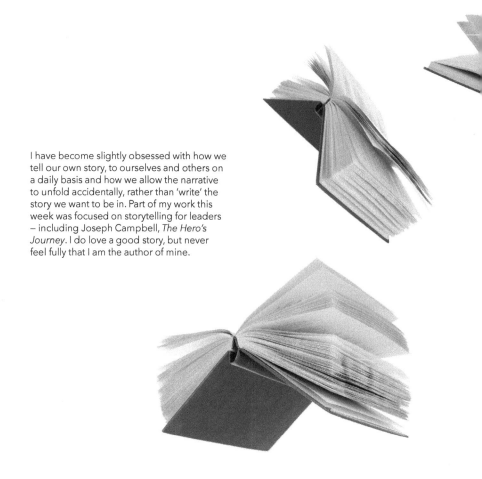

I have become slightly obsessed with how we tell our own story, to ourselves and others on a daily basis and how we allow the narrative to unfold accidentally, rather than 'write' the story we want to be in. Part of my work this week was focused on storytelling for leaders – including Joseph Campbell, *The Hero's Journey*. I do love a good story, but never feel fully that I am the author of mine.

NARRATIVE

love a story, new or old,
crafted well and clearly told,
I love when language paints a scene
More vivid than upon the screen,
I love those stories that inspire and move
And I love those that show how I might improve.
This week, dear listener, I've been immersed in fables
Discussing storytelling across business tables
We've Joseph Campbelled the Journey analogy
And we've considered history and mythology,
We've talked through themes, characters and plot,
Beginnings and endings, we've covered a lot!
We're encouraging leaders beyond information,
To seek the literary arts for inspiration
And at the heart of it all is one simple play,
That each of us holds a story in our head every day.
And rather than leaving that story to chance
We can consciously endeavour to lead that dance.
Create your own positive story, simply begin,
And construct a tale that you want to be in.
No matter what the novels on your shelf,
The most important narrative is the one you tell yourself.

A RANGE OF EMOTIONS

I had been working this week on 'The Agiles', a set of characters drawn as cartoons living inside your head. My childhood version was a cartoon strip called *The Numskulls*, the modern equivalent being the movie *Inside Out*. It spawned this idea of how emotions range around inside your mind.

Imagine a space, a range where things graze,
like you find in Oklahoma.
Except in the place of an animal's face
Emotions are the flora and fauna.
In a calm little corner ease and contentment
Are grazing side by side;
Whilst further afield, away from the others
Are emotions with pain inside.
There's sadness and mourning, disappointment, disgust,
Confused and frustrated kicking up dust.
Joy and euphoria are galloping free
Being chased by excited and 'thrilled to see.'
Chewing the cud, ambivalent, bored
Are, huh, hmm and meh—ignored.
Then there's a separate, staked-out pen
I reluctantly visit every now and again;
Inside are anger, suspicion, and rage,
Mistrust, fury, and harder to gauge,
Offended—strutting its stuff and making it clear,
No one's listening enough, except perhaps, fear.
This emotional savanna, this sentiment plain
Is full of our tempers in sunshine or rain
And all these feelings need pastoral care
You need to know when they're roaming out there
And where is this great farm with corral and shed?
Well you know, dear listener, it's inside your head.

PARTING IS SUCH SWEET SORROW

It seems poetry is the perfect medium for sadness; and I was sad, as our company's managing director, Danielle Thompson, left us for new adventures. I love the fact that as a company we made up a story to say she was just 'working at home,' so it would soften the blow of losing a friend – little did we know how prophetic that was. I said we would be proud to report our quarterly progress (Danielle is still a shareholder), and it turns out to be true.

People come and people go,
  Some quick-witted, others slow,
To get the gist, understand what it is we're trying to do;
People are our greatest asset, yes!
And while we're at it, they're also the biggest pain,
Then again, they're everything, aren't they?
Love them, hate them be frustrated,
Pleased, delighted, irritated,
They join your team so full of hope,
Their career, their talent, a kaleidoscope of possibilities.
Then come the trials and tribulations;
Situations you couldn't have dreamt of,
"They've gone where? She said what? I can't believe it!"
I can, as often I'm the man that did it first or worse.
It takes all kinds, so they say, diversity is the only way,
Some are stars that shine so bright
And some are wrong, and others right.
Some fit in and make the grade
Where others simply don't I'm afraid.
Some are stubborn, some are bold,
Some dynamic others old before their time.
Process driven, data mad,
Free thinking mavericks, I'm glad we've had them all.
Today we're sad, the wrench, the tear, the tears in our eyes and,
surprise! It's still hard,
Even though we've known for ages! Ahh, those Kubler-Ross stages,
But she's not really gone, she's simply moving on
And taking on, a new challenge.
So good luck Danielle, keep in touch,
We'll miss you very much.
But when you check in for your quarterly report,
We'll be proud to show you how well you taught us to
Run our business differently, efficiently, intelligently.
And we will rejoice in the choice you made… to be a monster.

I CAN'T
HEAR
YOU

2020 was shaping up to be a good year for the company, with many international events. With a busy schedule ahead, Jo and I gratefully accepted an offer of a short break with friends Rod and Janet in Austria. In the recording of the poem, against a mountain backdrop, I look very relaxed. Blissfully unaware of things to come and in a contemplative and reflective mood.

What a gift to listen to others. Be there—present—to lift spirits by your presence alone,
What if, mostly you think you're in sync? But your head is busy listening to itself, even on the phone!
There are three people in this conversation and two of them are me.
Are you really listening to this poetry?
How can we tell if we listen well or frustrate the voices lilting,
With the rate at which our concentration fades and decays like petals wilting?
"Yeah, I'm listening," I say during the day at work, but not without distraction.
Then later on, the conversation's stopped, and I notice a reaction.
"Why don't you listen to me when I'm talking?" "Al. Al. Put your phone away. Look at me,"
"Okay, okay. I'm here, I'm listening... definitely."
But it's not true, there are common barriers to hearing what's been said
Not just conversations, but also judgments in your head.
Don't value their opinion, their tone, their voice a whine,
Can't hear the song they sing, it's not in harmony with mine.
My head is nodding, I hear my voice saying 'yes' prompting them on
But a part of my mind is shouting, 'shut up, don't care, you're wrong!'
Other times I'm not engaged I'm simply paused, on hold,
I'm waiting for the moment to carry on with my gold.
I'm holding court, a storyteller of great renown
Don't stop me now, don't interrupt, you'll only bring me down;
Or like now, too tired to focus, it's not a good time to talk
Perhaps later, just us two, me and you; let's go for a walk.
Quality time, to establish a rhythm, sympatico—Perfect! There you go!
If you've made it this far, well then hurrah. You've listened well, that's neat,
But if you're up for it, try again; remove all distractions, empty your mind, repeat.
Do let me know, if you did and it sinks in.
In the wild, it's hard to know, if anyone's listening.

LOVE IS . . .

I performed this poem live at a local event in Leamington Spa on Valentine's day. The poem was inspired by those twee 70's illustrations, 'Love Is…', but there's plenty of raw emotion in the lines. I read that the artist, the late Kim Casali (nee Grove) drew them initially as notes to her future husband and was at one time earning $5-6 million per annum from the cartoons. She certainly spread a lot of love around the world.

Love is simple, love is kind,
Love is just a state of mind.
Love is awkward, love is tough,
Love is sometimes just enough.
Love can hurt you, love can bite,
Love can keep you up all night.
Love can smile, love can frown,
Love can sometimes let you down.
Love inspires, love misleads,
Love can lead you to misdeeds.
Love is aching, love is pain,
Love is lost yet love remains.
Love the dog, love my life,
Love my kids, love my wife (this week).
Love my work, I do, it's true.
Love writing: love, from me to you.
Love lots of stuff, love when you can.
Love is… the only plan.

The weekly deadline for the poems was a constant throughout the year and I was often 'late' according to my own schedule. Uploading the poems to LinkedIn, I'd noticed that if it was longer than one page, it was hard to read. This poem fitted onto one page easily. It's also a confession, hardly a secret, that I talk too much. Or rather, that I take too long to say what might be said more quickly.

BREVITY

My poems don't fit on LinkedIn;
They're either too fat or sometimes too thin.
It seems length is not a strength of mine,
I'm not known for my brevity,
I fare better, with levity.
I admit it, some of my verse is just too long,
I have a tendency to go on and on and on and on.
So, I rarely hear the sound of the gong
To get off.

LABELS

I'd just returned from a conference in Arizona, the last event we would facilitate that year, and a company called *Consciously Unbiased* was running sessions on unconscious bias and this was my response to their work. They liked it too, which was pleasing since they are experts in the field.

abels are helpful, labels are good.
They tell you what's plastic, tell you that's wood.
They tell you the name and make of a thing,
How to construct it and where to plug in.

Labels on clothing, labels on Spam,
On Marmite, cereals, on Grandma's plum jam.
Some labels are warnings, "Don't drink this bleach!"
"This Lilo won't save your life at the beach."

When labels are clear, they help and inform,
Tell medical staff when prem baby was born.
Smart labels for laptops, iPads and phones,
Handwritten labels on dug-up old bones

There's one set of labels no use at all;
Labels for humans, misleading and small.
No detailed instruction, no handle-with-care,
Too general, too sweeping, often not fair.

Introvert, extrovert, ENFJ,
Latino, Hispanic, bi, straight or gay.
These are just headings that get boxes ticked,
Don't let them define you, no don't be tricked.

You can decide to be he, she or they;
You can be you, in your own special way.
Each person's unique, no jar on a shelf.
If you'd like a label, write it yourself.

GOING

VIRAL

And so it began. By this time, the Covid-19 virus had been identified and was well on the move. There were already people saying we were making too much fuss; little did they or indeed any of us know at this point, just how it would play out.

VIRAL

VIRAL

VIRAL

VIRAL   VIRAL

VIRAL

AL

Bumping elbows, tapping feet,
Novel ways to meet and greet.
Cut-out hugging, don't shake hands,
Dark shadows across our lands.
Where we speak of going viral,
Replace this with a savage spiral,
Covid-19, growing unseen,
Our defence, quarantine.
A quiet killer, deadly foe,
Spreads quick, like blog or video.
No longer academic,
Maybe full pandemic!
Over-reaction, too much fuss?
Not sure that's how most of us
Are thinking. Are you scoffing?
Mocking those who are coughing?
Remember statistics are lives,
Sons, daughters, husbands, wives,
China, Italy, US, UK,
Numbers growing every day.
Ghostly cruise ships, empty flights,
Work being cancelled, sleepless nights.
Wuhan doctor—selfless man
Doing everything he can
To understand it, make it known;
He gave his life, the one, his own.
How many will pay that awful price?
Without his discovery, probably twice
As many, so I say let's do our best,
Wash our hands and all the rest,
To keep this thing at bay, away
From the vulnerable and the sick.
And if we do it well, we'll quickly
Be back at our festivals and meetings,
And returning to close friendly greetings.

OOOH LOOK, A BIRD!

An early indication that I am not entirely comfortable chained to a laptop. I am easily distracted at the best of times, so the idea of having to be locked in the same place all day saw me craving distractions.

There's just eight hours in the working day
And nothing is going to get in my way.
A lot to do, a proposal to send,
It needs to be completed by the end
Of the day, right, oh, there goes my phone.
It's probably Jo calling me from home;
No, it's just a message, WhatsApp I think,
Facebook messenger, do I want a drink
Tonight with Lee, if free? The Stag, at eight.
I could, maybe, but might need to work late.
If I crack on, I could have this thing done
By five, six at the latest, then gone
Out of here… ooh, email. LinkedIn update.
No, don't get distracted, just the click rate,
Comments, mentions, reacted, shares, liked,
Can't remember if I locked up my bike.
Oh, I've forgotten my lunch, home-made soup.
But what's this? Invitation to join a group?
Crikey Moses, it's half-past-ten,
I'll just get myself a coffee, maybe cake and then
Really get down to it, work flat out,
I ought to just give Robin a quick shout,
Oh wait, he's typing; Alana's typing;

Wonder what's happening, and now I'm typing.
And look, the best distraction of them all,
A double incoming video call.
It's past my lunchtime, I've got to go,
But yes of course I'll let you both know
My thoughts on the video. Right the deck
Mind you, sandwich first, because what the heck.
Health and wellbeing—don't forget
You have fitness targets to be met.
Now, settle down… calm… reflect,
Don't let anything deflect you from the, ooh,
Huff Post, Lad Bible, fun stuff in the news.
Write something onto Twitter, air my views,
Market, sell, say things are going really well,
Which is true they are but might not be now they've shut America!
What the…? No Europe entry, only exit,
UK's exempt, is that down to Brexit?
Oh my life, it's five o'clock, day nearly over
Check the to do list, haven't over-delivered
It's fair to say. Still, not on the breadline,
Don't think they'll mind, extending the deadline.
Tomorrow, yes. Focus will be the word,
Focus, focus, focus… ooh look, a bird!

WORKING FROM HOME

I had spent the week caring for my brother who was quite poorly, but not with Covid. Working remotely and video conferencing was nothing new to our company, but it was clearly becoming a challenge for many of our clients. We recorded this over Zoom and it was our way of saying, "It's okay, we're all in this together."

We're all familiar with working from home.
Video conferences—never home alone.
Step through this portal, come share our lives,
Meet partners, lodgers, pets, husbands and wives.
Whether on Skype, Teams, Adobe or Zoom,
You too can enter our collective front room.
I'm in the North, caring for my brother;
The feeling of being linked to each other
Is reassuring, joyful and alluring.
We love to connect, chat long and during
Calls we focus on stories, laughter, bants;
Of course, we joke about not wearing pants!
Work too: forecasts, reports, balances checks,
Progress on proposals, checking slide decks.
But rather than describe what is unseen,
Dear listeners, because of Covid -19
We thought we would share hearth, table and rug,
And send all our friends a virtual hug.

Robin. I'm in Essex, close to the sea,
With Connie the Westie, and just home for tea.
Caroline, College exec; absent children, two:
Lily—Harvard, Barney—actor, who knew?

Georgina, that's me, Northern like Alan,
Good humour; have energy by the gallon.
Two wonderful children, both still in school,
I love virtual working, as a rule.

Alana, the artist, the visual one,
Whatever style artwork, I get it done;
I love my work, using creative skills.
Rob, my bearded husband—whisky distills.
Our dog Murphy won't be joining this call;
Last week was farewell to a friend loved by all.

I'm here, I'm new, Hilary, H to you,
My role: to keep finance clearly in view.
Only a few weeks in; I have a cat;
These dog lovers are just getting used to that

The very best thing in our virtual space?
Befriending people all over the place.
Mike and his film crew, and Craig on graphics,
Technology's better than telepathics.
For our global friends we don't need a Tardis
To say "hi" to Betsey and Kate Georgiades,
Oksana, Nataliya, Russ, Sarah, brought close,
Osly, Gerd, Shungu, and not only those,
MCL Jamie, Elinor—accounts.
A world virtually-connected amounts
To something in our unwritten book;
We've glimpsed their lives, taken a good look
At what matters. Let yourself be known.
Join in, be seen, embrace working from home.
Maybe, at first, it's to avoid infection,
Now let's make this the greatest connection.
Sign up, video on, kids' faces besmudged;
Join the great hangout and be unjudged.

Photos of Robin, George and Alana by Dave Perry Photography

INSIDE OUT

I've used the Disney Pixar movie *Inside Out* many times as a way of considering how we manage our emotions. I love the idea that there are a cast of characters in your head, operating the console of your life. During lockdown, they seem to be especially active.

Inside our heads, are characters playing
And Jostling for position, each one saying
How we should behave and how we might feel.
Disney's artists beautifully reveal
Five core emotions, lovingly drawn;
With us from the very moment we're born.
There's Anger, Joy, Sadness, Disgust and Fear,
The fact we have them all is crystal clear.
Impossible now to keep them at bay,
In this clamped-down world, they'll have their say.

Our emotions on show, the best, the worst;
Do share what yours say, why don't I go first.

Fear for people's futures, damaged, lost,
Fear for failing businesses' human cost,
Fear Coronavirus, truly, fear death,
Fear the hospital bed—fighting for breath.

Joy at the sight of sunshine, spring begun,
Joy for laughter, online Zooming fun,
Joy for the generous spirit of giving,
Joy for the unbounded joy of living.

Sad for the families that are torn apart,
Sad, such sad stories, don't know where to start.
Sadness is healing as much as it's pain,
Sadness we meet you again and again.

Joy for family unexpected together,
Joy for unusual English weather.

Angry with idiots ignoring warnings,
Disgusted with my wasted mornings.
Angry that health workers couldn't buy food,
Disgusted with shoppers being rude.
Angry with Harry, dislocating shoulder,
Angry that I'm hurting—getting older,
Angry that I'm writing so late at night,
Angry that I'm… hold it, hold it… right.

Joy when I get out to cycle on my bike,
Joy at poetic shares or a poetic like.

In the film emotions run your console,
To determine when you're a saint, or an arsehole.
No use pretending that Joy is in charge
When up jumps Anger, or Sadness looms large.
Notice emotions, don't try to lock them down;
Grit teeth, clench fists, stamp foot, sigh, smile, frown.
And whilst you're stuck at home, can't get about,
Please watch the movie, Disney's Inside Out.
It's meant for kids, but it's insightful, rich,
And can help keep you sane, when life's a bitch.
Internet, or standing, distanced in line,
You balance your emotions, I'll balance mine.

This was a mantra that I had been espousing for a long time. We deal with many global clients and I am always surprised by the amount of people who don't want to turn their camera on. The pandemic has done a great deal to encourage the use of cameras, but I have also understood more and respect those that don't necessarily feel as comfortable as I do on screen. I do however stick with my prediction that we'll be doing this for a long, long, long time.

TURN YOUR CAMERA ON

Don't be afraid, turn your camera on
I mean come on, what could possibly go wrong?
As long as your face is in mostly in view
You can comfortably chat with one or two
Or 200, if that's the size of group
With Teams, Zoom or Skype you stay in the loop
One or two watch-outs, you might like to know
Otherwise, get out there, give it a go
Etiquette's your choice, try not to eat food
Tell others first if you're appearing nude
Try not to be texting, sexting or typing
Nor screens, faces or bottoms wiping
Hoovers, doorbells, pets, kids, tolerate
Occupational hazards and any rate
The more you attempt to keep them quiet
It's most guaranteed you'll start a riot.
Mute, unmute, mute, unmute, just do your best
Stay abreast of the conversation, lest
You lose track of who is talking. Avoid
Leaving the room, folks might get annoyed
And if during your call, your screen should freeze
Well, log out, log in, out, in again and please
Try to use headphones, because an echo
Is unsettling, breaks concentration "Oh
Is that me? Sorry, some setting I've chosen
Hang on I think the screen may have frozen"
Modern platforms, interact, fun and games
Message, chat, share screens, change backgrounds, change names
Just doesn't matter if you get stuff wrong
We'll be doing this for a long, long, long
Time. So cast fears aside, jump in the pool
And turn your camera on, that's the only rule.

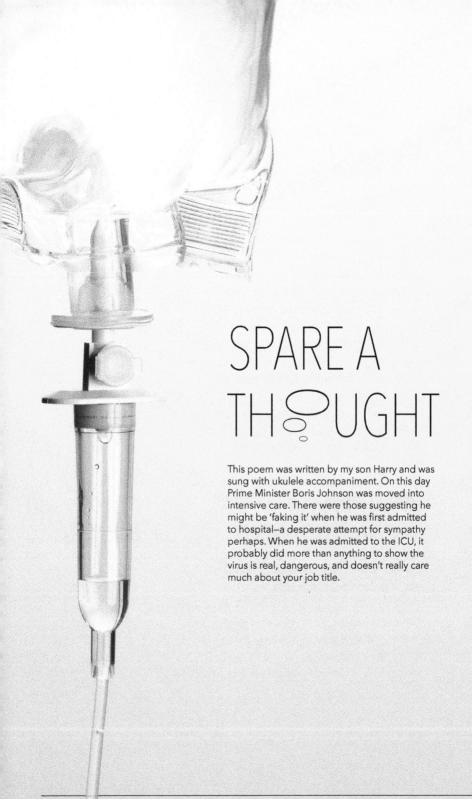

SPARE A
TH O UGHT

This poem was written by my son Harry and was
sung with ukulele accompaniment. On this day
Prime Minister Boris Johnson was moved into
intensive care. There were those suggesting he
might be 'faking it' when he was first admitted
to hospital—a desperate attempt for sympathy
perhaps. When he was admitted to the ICU, it
probably did more than anything to show the
virus is real, dangerous, and doesn't really care
much about your job title.

Spare a thought for doctors
In the NHS.
Spare a thought for nurses,
They're doing their level best.

Supermarket workers
And those manning the phones.
Those with jobs, those without them,
Those who live home alone.

Delivery drivers, bakers,
The anxious and bereaved;
When we make it to the end of this
There'll be time to feel relieved.

Spare a thought for the homeless,
Those plagued by mental health,
Everyone who's struggling,
And don't forget yourself.

Though businesses are hampered,
Most things are getting through.
The food, heat, light and water Co.
They spare a thought for you.

Spare a thought for Boris,
He has COVID-19.
The virus can take anyone,
Stay in and quarantine.

Think of those schooling at home
And those who read the news,
For high rise dwellers with little space
And those who collect our refuse.

Spare a thought for parents
And those who closed their caffs,
And for the singers, players and comics
Online providing laughs.

There's still a way to go,
Mental battles to be fought,
So sit back, take a breath,
And remember, spare a thought.

WHAT ARE YOU WAITING FOR?

As was often the case, this poem was an emotional response to something I'd read. I am all in favour of learning and self-development, but sometimes the pressure to 'be the best you' is just plain irritating. When so many of us, myself included, were struggling with mental health, it was time to take care and be gentle to your psyche, rather than perish in the pursuit of perfection.

Are you learning piano, violin, guitar?
Bagpipes, flute, ukulele, sitar?
Carpe diem, the online coaches say,
Don't sit there idle, don't dare waste a day.

If you've been furloughed, act now, grab your chance.
First learn to juggle, and then ballroom dance,
Work out with Wicks, then it's yoga at 10,
Mindfulness, calm meditation… Zen.

But no relaxing, no bingeing tv,
If you haven't already, update your cv.
Set targets, goals, start a business right now.
Get online, stay online, all night somehow.

Join a network and take up live streaming,
Don't be satisfied with low level dreaming.
Plan big, aim high, write a book, make a pile.
Get off your arse and do something worthwhile.

Painter, poet, maybe business guru,
The only thing holding you back is you.
Find your purpose, be a great composer,
Bring your best life that little bit closer.

A great journey begins with just one step;
Get up, get a life, get a grip, get pep!
Carpentry, pottery, baking a cake.
Just choose something… for goodness sake!

Do it, strike now before it's too late;
There's hundreds ready at the starting gate.
Don't fall behind it's the last chance saloon,
Soar up, soar up in your gilded balloon.

Nah, I don't buy it, it's actually ok
You don't have to do any of that today.
Let go of the guilt, be kind to yourself,
Put that crap business book back on the shelf.

Whatever the influencers have to say
You can just take your time, live day by day.
For whether with others or all alone,
You've achieved so much, simply staying at home.

This poem was clearly fashioned after the Marriott Edgar monologues of my youth, recorded by Stanley Holloway – *Three Ha'pence a Foot* was the first thing I ever performed at senior school. Edgar wrote many of the monologues about historical figures, real and imagined, so St George's Day provided a good opportunity to share the story of our company's resilience. My father could recite most of these monologues, whilst accompanying himself on the piano. 'E were reet good 'n' all.

ST GEORGE AND THE MONSTERS

Let me tell you an everyday story
To which some of you might relate.
Of a creative company in Britain,
You know, where it's small, but Great.

Purple Monster is the name of our team,
Conferences our bread and butter,
an ill wind, that blows no one any good
Has caused our business to stutter.

Sweeping through the land, Armageddon all but
Put the kibosh on plans this year.
No flights, no hotels, no gathering in groups,
We're going nowhere soon, oh dear!

So, what to think, what's to do whilst we're stuck?
There's no use fretting for nowt.
We 'ave to face the brutal reality,
Stop in, stay at home, don't go out.

But the business can't sleep, has to crack on,
Got to flex, adapt and pivot.
Like learning to play virtual golf online,
Same swing, just don't take a divot.

So we've shifted, we've switched, we're all on screen
Zooming, Teaming, Robin and Me.
It turns out our old career was helpful,
Acting up on children's tv.

It's times like these that your values count;
Kindness, trust, loyalty and fun;
And with the help of our clients and friends,
We're getting the online job done

Just like St George, when he beat that dragon,
You have to play to your strengths,
You have to believe in yourself and your team
And know that they'll go to all lengths.

What twists and turns, which path will we take?
What challenges will we weather?
Whatever the way, I'll be proud to say,
"We've all of us done it together."

This week I had seen one of many articles about wildlife wandering into cities and towns across the world as the pandemic kept people indoors. Goats and deer in Welsh towns seemed less dangerous than bears and pumas elsewhere. So too had the cleaner air become apparent with the lack of traffic on the road. It made me consider other good outcomes that might arise from the change of lifestyle forced upon us by the virus. As I look back now, from '21, I am encouraged by a number of changes that seem to be sticking.

A NEW REALITY

There's a point, approaching slowly, where a threshold will be crossed.
Where we'll leave this lockdown world and the loved ones that we've lost.
We may return to normal, whatever that might be,
But what that looks or feels like, no one can quite agree.
Has our world changed forever? It hasn't stopped revolving,
Yet I sense an opportunity, for societal evolving.
Leaving transformation to chance doesn't seem right or smart,
So here's a few handy hints, to help leaders know where to start.

Working from home, seems mostly a plus, flexible working's key.
And conference calls can be just fine, with kids or pets on your knee.
We're not returning to 9-5, we need working lives built with space
For family, fun, personal time, so perspective has its place.
We'd like more women leaders, the evidence undeniable;
I'm afraid men-only's had its day, 100% unreliable.
We'd love less traffic in the town, for the smog to fade away,
To breathe clean air and prove greenhouse gas has had its day.
Bears and elephants in the street might not be the desired state,
but sustainable living's the goal for all, before it proves too late.
A big hurrah for companies who stepped up in time of need,
Putting community and saving lives ahead of self or greed.
Boo to those whose values meant, only selfish needs were met;
And remember when we spend again, that our dollars won't forget.
Let's not praise frontline workers now, then forget them when trouble's passed;
Let's make changes for the best and make those changes last.
Nurses, teachers, restaurant staff, those stacking supermarket shelves,
They deserve to earn a decent living, enough to be themselves.
There's a gap between the rich and poor, that's not just based on wealth,
It's the opportunities to learn, to live and bank upon good health.
So who will build this better future? Is it all just so much talk?
Will our leaders be the ones who truly walk the walk?
Who will boldly venture and change the status quo?
What's the new reality, which direction do we go?
We all know the answer to who creates a better way,
It's each and every one of us, each and every day.

CREATIVE THINKING

Like everyone else, holiday plans for the week were cancelled, but we had unexpected fun using WhatsApp to create an imaginary golf tour. I love creativity and our company thrives upon it, and it seems to flow best when it starts with playfulness. I don't fancy spending every holiday in the backyard, but it was a laugh.

This week, the first in May, I was supposed to be on vacation,
But like most of the population, I remained at my workstation.
No chance to travel, no aeroplanes to board,
The back yard the only destination the virus will afford.
16, mature (ish) men, off golfing, annual tour
But no golf clubs would be packed, no foot stepped out the door.
Next year perhaps, but wait, what could save the situation?
Overcome the problem—what about… imagination?
Yes, the four-day break is off, no golf, no drinks, no group activity,
But with WhatsApp chat, no travel's needed, just creativity.
For four days we entertained each other with postings of imaginary games,
Incredible shots, holes in one, the leader board with all our names,
And when the annual shindig was over, turns out I'd lost again.
But next year we'll be in Ireland for real, I'll try to win it then.
Creativity is a powerful force, and we should use it more;
Business leaders let it in, when it comes knocking at your door.
During the lockdown I've observed, it's been an oft employed tool.
Here's just a few of the things, creativity has solved, kind of cool
When we needed hand sanitizer and let's be honest a bit less gin,
The distillers of our country creatively stepped in.
When we needed solutions for the breathlessness we feared,
Engineers used creative thinking and fresh ventilators appeared.
When we needed PPE and just had to find a way,
Dressmakers designed scrubs patterns, creatively saving the day.
When the kids are bored at home and you have to entertain,
Inventing quizzes, games and kitchen sports—creativity wins again.
When there's no concerts, theatre, comedy gigs, when nothing live is shown,
The creative urge to sing, to dance, means we create our own.
Fine art is blooming, playing guitar, online classes in opera too.
If it's what you fancy, and you've time, welcome the creative you.
When your birthday party's cancelled because your friends can't come around,
Enjoy the drive-by honking crew a brand-new party sound.
When the local pub has closed (it has) with a serious funding gap,
How about creating a crowd-funding page, to ensure future beer's on tap?
A Harvard professor, described this week, crisis management in words so clear,
He called it rapid innovation, under stress, embedded in fear.
Whatever the challenge, great or small, every neighbourhood, every nation
Has an incredible resource, a route to the most effective innovation.
In my humble opinion, each and every human has a natural proclivity,
When push comes to shove and all else is lost, we still have creativity.

INVE$TM£NT ADVICE

It was my wife Jo's 60th birthday on the 14th and I was lucky enough to be able to arrange a virtual birthday performance of songs from West End shows, from lots of showbiz friends. They were just brilliant in the way they rallied around and got a great job done. Jo is very social and has found missing friends as tough as anyone and it made her day to see how many people cared. Ahh.

This week has been fun, with moments of stress.
Friends recording songs from Barnum and Chess.
It was Jo's birthday, so much to arrange,
But no party venue, peculiar, strange.
Each person singing and filming from home,
Uploads and downloads from cameras and phones.
A zoom call arranged, 40 folks online,
But not sure the film can render in time.
The call has started, the film's not ready,
Just fill for a bit, keep your nerve, steady.
Chat with some guests like a radio show
And wait for Matt to say yes, and press go.
It went off fine, a bit seat of the pants;
Great film, great songs and one sofa dance.
At the heart of it all something so dear,
Longstanding friendships built over the years.
We've been through loads—laughed and cried together;
Trials, tribulations, weathered weather.
Same for us at work, contracts rarely end
'Cos we're in the business of making friends.
These times are hard, the small business juggle;
It's hand-to-mouth a familiar struggle.
But whenever it's tough, have friends on call,
They'll help you, they're on your side, that's all.
If you need to separate real from trends,
Don't rely on social, rely on friends.
I don't often give investment advice
But for this top tip, I don't have to think twice,
Invest in relationships, lasting bonds—
Not the gilt-edged type, but those that go beyond.
Transactions and bring returns far above
Invest in friends, the ROI is love.

This poem was written to mark Mental Health Awareness Week and I really enjoyed creating the video of the recitation, with a split screen talking to myself. I know that we all have an inner voice, but seeing it brought to life on the screen was helpful, to me at least. I don't think anyone on the planet can really have gone through 2020 without some challenges to their mental health and sharing problems and reaching out to others seems to be one line of defence.

MENTAL SELF HEALTH

A poem this week concerning mental health;
a dialogue, twixt me and my inner self.
Welcome to inner Alan——shadow-side——
The character I, we, usually hide.

> *Well this is new, speaking out loud at last.*
> *Troubling, I'm not normally part of the cast.*
> *Sure you want to lay inner workings bare?*
> *Reveal real thoughts, I urge caution, take care.*

Might be good, to hear from my evil twin.
So, negative me, why don't you begin?

> *Don't blame me when you get, no likes, no shares,*
> *It's LinkedIn, not the real world, no one cares.*
> *You're not a proper poet, it's business stuff;*
> *You'll never be published, you're not good enough.*

There he is, constantly chipping away;
Unwelcome head guest, in here every day.
I wonder what purpose it is you serve,
Does each of us get the voice we deserve?

> *You think my job's easy? Subconscious thought*
> *Bearing scars from emotional battles fought?*
> *Mine the angst, anger, fear, take all the blows*
> *You repress, blame me for depressive lows!*
> *The problems of the mind are persistent*
> *And you rarely ask for assistance.*

Why never upbeat, no silver lining,
Why always harping on, carping, whining?
One of us has to say things are going well.

Have you learnt nothing from therapy, hell?!
You hide your woes with a brave or silly face.

Yes that's right I do, both of them have their place.

Shallow Al, seek purpose not distraction,
Life must be meaningful, for satisfaction.

Like all great critics, you are the best advisor
But always from the back seat, never driver.
I face the world, my ideas win or die.

Oh please, where's success? You're barely getting by.
You think you should beat this crisis alone,
Idiot, too stubborn to pick up the phone.
Ask your friends for help, no stiff upper lip;
Drop the mantra, 'get a grip,' 'get a grip.'
Instead, let go, relax, and ease our mind,
Take the week's national theme, and... be kind.

To who?

To you.

To me?

To you.

To me.
That seemed somehow familiar, but yes, I see.
Peace of mind is a treasure we both need,
If we achieve that, we are rich indeed.
I wish you all a tranquil state of mind,
And remember to yourself, be most kind.

W_____ F____ M_

I read Brian Bilston's poem, 'Roger's Thesaurus' and I realised there is no need to torture myself when I'm unable to think of a word – which is very, very often. That said however, I did try and seek help from the thesaurus and a rhyming dictionary, but in the end, both slowed me down, so I carried on writing without them. It probably shows. Words fail me!

Picture this: You're peckish and you just put your money into a vending machine.
   You lean in, with anticipation, to watch the metal spiral inch your snack towards you,
Any moment now, the chocolate bar will land and be in your hand.
Unwrapped before you can say… before you can say… what's happening, it hasn't dropped!
It's stopped on the edge, stuck on the ledge, it's not falling. Oh.
That is the feeling I get when I'm searching for words, they're perching just out of reach,
Or words are birds, fluttering whilst I'm stuttering, spluttering and grasping thin air.
There's nothing there, at least not where it should be, where I can easily take it and place it
On my page, am I at an early stage of something serious or is it just my age?
I've entered my 7th decade, bits decaying, ageing, blood thinning, winning less important,
But when words fail me, it ails me that I can't recall the name, the place, the day, the way
Things happened, as others can who keep a picture in their minds eye.
Why, O why, can't I?
Robin and I play a game, where I describe the film, the action, the character, the plot
And then he names it. We play it a lot, recently and he, decently is a sport
And doesn't make me feel bad, for my failure to name Julia Roberts or Josh Gad,
But I have hit a bit more of a problem, because I'm writing these lines
And each week complete rhymes and need words to be there for me
Easily in reach so I can teach, preach, charm, encourage and cajole my listeners.
And with each passing week, I've noticed it getting harder, the same words are in my literary larder
(Literary larder!) See what I mean, I'm stuck, in a wordless rut, but…
…someone has come to my aid and made it possible to expand my range.
Charlie the Tall Photographer, yes, he. Sending out each week, his Five Good Things missive,
And this is where I've found salvation, a poetic oration by one Brian Bilston—poet.
And though it irks me to realize help was always at hand, it took him to remind me
That I should simply stand up, walk to the bookshelf and take down Roget's Thesaurus,
Where I will find a chorus (or massed choir perhaps) of words (type, print, copy, characters),
You get the idea. No worry about my fading memory, inability to recall
Because all the time, I'll have this by my side. And when my mind is fishing
Wishing like mad it could remember the right word, I'll turn to this and won't forget
A single thing again, and yet… I have a niggling worry… but best hurry, or I'll miss my deadline.

've started this poem about a hundred times
And found it difficult to write the lines.
Should I even be trying to add my voice
To the cacophony of sound? My choice
I guess but to what end? What will it avail?
The opinion of one so white, so pale?
But nothing can come from nothing—silence.
I don't need a corporate poet's licence
To speak from the heart, to tell you how I feel.
Appalled, ashamed, saddened, forlorn, I kneel
To the memory of George Floyd—say his name.
I hope from now we'll never be the same.
I see my privilege, supremacy too.
I'm with Ben and Jerry's cause, are you?

This is June 6th, the week after
the death of George Floyd – say
his name. Interesting in hindsight
what I put about Trump, but most
striking is the raw feeling, and
that it felt appropriate to kneel
during the recording. A friend
dropped me a note to say they
were proud to be my friend after
seeing the video.

Dismantle the system, rotten, decayed,
Can't be fixed, it's the way it was made.
I think corporate leaders can pave the way;
Diversity and equity every day.
Root out racism, check out our bias,
If we don't live the values, fire us.
We'll know when prejudice is defeated,
Every top table, with black leaders seated.
I stood in the park for a while today,
I heard what people of colour had to say.
Our majority-white middle-class town
Saw five hundred people or more kneel down.
Mutterings from some and their 'all lives' cliché.
They don't accept white privilege do they?

The law can be a very different thing
Depending on the colour of your skin.
When I was young, stopped by police speeding,
I'd get a caution before proceeding.
Where prejudice and racism is rife,
A young black driver must fear for their life.
If they hear a siren and see the blues,
They're not the ones who're privileged to choose.
The conversation and what happens next,
They might get a cop kneeling on their neck!
It's outrageous, disgusting, has to stop,
But don't have faith in the bloke at the top.
A man outside a church, bible waving,
Preaching mostly violence, ranting, raving;
Around him citizens, angry, seething.
Policemen killed George, stopped him from breathing.
Protesting is right, protest day and night,
Protest until every person who's white
Acknowledges that they have a part in the how
It should change, and that they'll start that change now.
For nine minutes today, stop all white chatter,
Loudly, proudly say "Black Lives Matter."

GO AHEAD...
MAKE MY DAY

George Floyd's funeral took place in Houston; protests at his death were widespread across the globe; a statue of a slave trader was torn down and thrown into the docks in Bristol. I, amongst many, am hopeful that George Floyd's tragic death will bring about lasting change. I took part in a local protest, my first. This poem captured a moment in the local park, where a young black man commented on my recently-dyed purple hair.

A young black man just made my day.
Shouting across the park to me, "Hey!"
I observed the youth and a smile returned.
I continued with my dog, unconcerned
But he pursued engagement, calling out
And pointing at my head, a further shout
"Your hair!" I'd forgotten in this daylight view
How richly purple are my locks—their hue.
"Ah yes," I said, "My lockdown look,
"My daughter's idea," but really, I took
The decision to make a change I could control
Rather than accept a 'done to' victim role.
Then braided, beaded, still at school,
He raised me up, blessed and gifted me with, "Cool."

DIGITAL NATIVE

Our lives are digital, it's a numbers game.
Ones, zeros and ones, we're all the same.
Are you an Android, Windows, Chrome, Mac?
The future's numerical, there's no turning back.
Alarm in the morning, no chime starts the day;
Phone, glowing and buzzing, liquid crystal display.
That first touch-screen moment, a brush or stroke,
Remember when that was how lovers awoke?
Step out of bed, open bathroom door,
Digital timer warms tiled bathroom floor.
Toothbrush is programmed, sonic sensors hum
Around the mapped contour of tooth and gum,
Shower—controlled, gas, electric smart meters,
Dressed and downstairs, here's Siri to greet us.
The cereal box, bar code displayed;
Machines tracing end-to-end trade.
Supply chain data, transacted, approved,
Optimized algorithms, ordered it moved.
When you've finished your snap, crackle and pop,
It's time to start work and open the laptop.
The numbers cascade, flooding your brain,
Posing as stories of pleasure and pain.
Webinars, vlogs, podcasts and more,
Streaming data, through fibre to core.
Glue your face to the screen, lean in,
Mesmerized by pixels and pages within.
This is your workday, your purpose and cause,
No space for humans, no time to pause.
We used to drink coffee, in real cafés;
Not now in this Covid-led digital phase.
But surely, real soon, we'll be back in play,
There'll be people and laughter, human contact each day.

But wait, the bean counter's been counting, the numbers are in,
Stay home, sell the office, no travel, win-win.
Muwahahaha, the CFOs laugh.
We make the same profit and cut costs in half.
Proclaim the good news from the tallest tower,
We can watch numbers going up hour by hour.
Is this all there is? Is this what work means?
Changing a series of numbers on screens?
Let's pivot, shift, now is the time.
Time for a change to the old bottom line.
It's a digital world, from that we can't hide,
But let's measure what we treasure, you decide.
Have fun, from spreadsheets unencumbered,
And remember, ultimately, all our days are numbered.

I'm sure someone has written it before, but I was quietly pleased with "…bean counter's been counting," and it struck a chord with our accountants too. As I write these notes in 2021, we are investing in a permanent virtual broadcast studio, and one major selling point is cost saving. I do hope, post Covid, that we will begin to look beyond numbers when it comes to what businesses can achieve for their staff, customers and the wider community.

POETRY IN MOTION

A chance conversation with my physiotherapist revealed some fascinating local history. On February 23rd, 1847, Frederick Douglass spoke at the Music Hall in Bath Street, and Spencer Street Chapel in my hometown of Leamington Spa, Warwickshire. It seemed fitting to create a poem about the history of the town, which I filmed on my bicycle, to celebrate the visit of renowned abolitionist Douglass.

We're coming out of lockdown, slowly blinking in the sun.
Cautiously emerging, a small revival has begun.
Shops opening blinds, removing signs from doors.
People getting out and about, seeing them more and more.
Leamington's Parade, minor majestic regency view.
In the early 1900's, this top part of town was new,
The Regent Hotel, named after a Prince, later George the Fourth
Queen Victoria, who we'll meet as I cycle south, from north,
The Town Hall, 'Death in Leamington,' poet: Betjeman, John.
There she is, though her plinth is wonky, a wartime bomb.
Now the grandest part, the Royal Pump Rooms and Baths,
A historic memento of our Royal Spa Town past.
And the opposite side are the Jephson garden gates,
Named in the doctor's honour, marked by plaques and plates.
As we cross the bridge the grandeur starts to fade;
Enter into old town, leave behind the columned palisade.
All Saints Church, slowly crumbling, acid, eating stone.
Turn right at Vialli's kebab shop, where you rarely eat alone.
Down the back of the bins and into Spencer Yard,
No one to meet this cycling solitary bard.
But these stones could tell some tales, they've been here ages;
Hosted dignitaries, politicians, soldiers, poets, sages.
Here's one to remember, an orator behind that wall,
In 1847, an American abolitionist filled the Congregational Hall.
The most famous Frederick Douglass, activist renowned
Delivered a rousing speech in our little town.
Is he well remembered, is there a statue on the site?
No, not even a whisper of his speech that February night!
He did more to change people's lives than any local mayor,
He campaigned against slavery, taught freedom, right there.
But it's not in the history tour, nothing written on the brick,
Keep black history hidden, that's the colonial's trick.
Not here, not now, this story is out,
And like George Floyd, his name deserves a shout.
So in honour of this leader, on behalf of my small town,
I shall call his name and let it echo round.
FREDERICK DOUGLASS.

OFF
DOWN
THE
PUB

On the 4th July, the government eased the lockdown restrictions and allowed people, amongst other things, to go back to the pub. It went against scientific advice and probably common sense. The pubs closed again in the second national lockdown in November and haven't opened since. As I write these notes, we have passed 125,000 deaths in the UK from Covid-19. It's nothing to do with pubs specifically, but they are part of the national psyche and one example of how we have – in my humble opinion – so badly managed the pandemic here in the UK.

We've really been through the mill recently, all of us put to the test,
At times like these, there's only one solution "Landlord: a pint of your best."
The trouble is, the pubs have been shut, there's been nowhere to run or hide;
Nowhere to obtain that sense of safety you get when you walk inside.
The British pub is an institution, a safe haven of calm and peace—
Apart from a Saturday night in town when it's crawling with police.
Our relationship with the drink goes back hundreds of years:
Romans, Vikings, taverns, inns, gin, more gin… beers.
A place of refuge and rest, some vittles, a bed and the booze,
Your money and your memory, both overnight you can lose.
But because they've been closed, pandemically locked,
We've been deprived of this comfort, our senses shocked.
We don't do therapy, or soak in the tub,
When we've got a problem, we go down the pub.
We can chat and drink and drink and chat, and drink,
Then we drink some more, fall about a bit and think.
We think of important things like, who bought the last drink,
Then we drinky think and thinky drink and wait for the lock-in,
Draw the curtains, dim the lights, ignore the law, it's shocking!
Our local is one of the best, a proper community pub;
Generous hosts, Mandy and Trefor, have made it a social hub.
When forced to close its doors, neighbours raised thousands of pounds.
It seemed right to lend a hand, like buying a supportive round.
Saturday is the 4th of July—Independence Day—
Millions will throng the streets and shout hooray.
But this is no salute to an independent nation,
Just a trip to the pub, an act of desperation?
You see Covid is still here, so sneakily I know
In my heart of hearts, I shouldn't really go.
Government isn't acting with empathy, take note:
They've done it so the populace will remember when they vote.
"The PM has opened pubs again, he's the man, let's drink to him."
But medically, scientifically, their reasoning is thin.
You make up your own mind, as I reach bottom of my page,
Here's the advice from the scientists of SAGE:
It's not yet safe for groups to meet indoors,
2 metres apart we recommend, the choice is yours.
If there is a fatal shift, numbers once more rising up,
It will be an awful price to pay for an hour down the pub.

THE MASK

t appears there's some reluctance for people to wear a mask—
Understandable, it's a change for all, but is it such a big ask?
I thought for our encouragement and health education,
I'd consider some famous mask-wearers for elucidation.
If we can see what face coverings can achieve,
It might help us take that step—our anxieties relieved.
Let's start with Batman, a superhero, no one's fool.
His mask has pointy ears, sharp nose piece, pretty cool,
But I'm sorry to say, as protection goes, he's missed the mark.
The mouth is totally exposed and although he can see in the dark
It offers no help when it comes to the virus, not so much as a gauze.
I'm sorry, it may hide your identity Bruce, but you're a lost cause.
Catwoman fares no better, though if I'm honest, she looks a real cool cat.
She hasn't covered any of her face at all, you've got to do better than that!
The Joker? I don't know where to start, it isn't a mask, just paint;
You may be laughing on the other side of your face, but safe? You ain't.
Others have failed to grasp the simple principle of a cover:
The Phantom of the Opera, for example, what happened to the other
Half of the thing? Too busy keeping Christine in her place
To do a proper job of covering his whole face.
The Elephant Man, it's just some sacking, but he was lacking means.
And Hannibal Lecter, that's no face protector, could still eat fava beans.
What about The Mask Jim Carrey wore? Magical and made of wood.
Nope, wonderful dancing, terrific cartoons, but for Covid-19, no good…
So, who's got it right, who's bettered the caped crusader?
Look no further, than arch villain himself, yes, Lord Vader.
Not only has he got it right, but his leadership's super-duper.
Those under his command, thousands of safe stormtroopers.
It's got a built-in filter, but it isn't quite what we're seeking;
That's because as we know, it's very hard to hear him speaking.
But there is one role model, upon whom we can all rely
And that is… Spider-Man. Let me tell you why:

The covering is 100 per cent, no gaps, no holes, no faults,
He's tested it under extreme conditions, as over buildings he vaults.
He always wears his mask in public, removes it only now and then
In his support bubble, with Auntie May, Mary Jane or Gwen.
He knows that it's a courtesy, protecting others where you can from harm;
Seeing that covered friendly face, brings a sense of calm.
It's not just his web slinging, fighting or agility,
It's the fact that he accepts and takes responsibility.
Tom Hanks this week, urged us all to carry out three simple tasks:
Social-distance, wash your hands and wear a mask.
If it's good enough for Tom, it's good enough for me.
Have a great weekend everyone, virus free.

This week saw Tom Hanks take to video to announce he had no respect for anyone that couldn't do three 'tiny things:' Wear a mask, wash their hands and social-distance. Tom was in a great place to give advice since he had contracted Covid-19 whilst filming in New Zealand. I guess one of my all-time favourite film stars talking about masks led me to explore mask-wearing films stars. If there is one place that seems to be handling Covid as badly as the UK, it's the US.

Just one of many days where 'pivoting' the business felt like carrying a double-wardrobe upstairs on your own. It's hard, kind of ridiculous, and you know you should get help. My eldest brother's bouncebackability is often a source of inspiration and is for this poem. As I write this in 2021, we have properly reinvented Purple Monster as a virtual company, and we are firmly on our feet. I'm very grateful for that and recognize that is not the picture for everyone. Honestly, writing the poems genuinely helped me cope with change and disruption. Who knew?

ONCE MORE UNTO THE BREACH

Oh woe is me, sad day, alas alack!
Someone give me my precious old life back.
Once more to jet around the world with friends
And through conferences, meetings, meet 'our ends.'
Us, on our feet, facilitating fun,
A thrill-filled year ahead, great business won.
Then wham, or more accurately Wuhan;
Our destiny, no longer ours to plan!
A skidding, shuddering stuttering halt;
Something about a horse, stable and bolt.
Too late, virus racing cross country and town,
Forcing everyone home and into lockdown.
Jump forward to now, the present-day scene:
Staring at lap-top with hands overclean.
"Pivot," they said, "and reinvent yourself,
Don't be that company left on the shelf."
Business is booming, right sector, right place;
Innovate, move forward, pick up the pace.

But what if I'm tired, worn out, weary?
Every day starts with mind and eyes bleary.
We've reconstructed ourselves times before,
And scraped each other off catastrophe's floor.
Surely we don't have to do it again, not now!
Tell me there's someone who has a clue, how?
Oh suck it up babe, less of the whining:
Resilience, dig deep, silver lining.
Once more unto the breach dear friends, once more;
A rallying cry heard somewhere before.
What doesn't kill you makes you stronger—Nietzsche.
These painful life lessons are there to teach you,
You've got this, you can do it, you're the man;
Barack and Michelle Obama: Yes We Can.
But some days it feels like a heavy load.
Not sure the journey's worth it on this road.
But whenever I feel like packing it in,
I remember my brother, who lives in Hua Hin.
His businesses have crashed before you see,
Some of them, quite spectacularly.
Just happened again; picking up pieces
His determination never ceases
To amaze me and everyone he meets
To get up from the knockouts, the defeats.
He's the spirit of Asterix the Gaul,
And he's only 5ft 5 inches tall.
He's reinvented himself, plastic free.
A cleaner world his business legacy,
His energy, excitement, hope for all,
An eco-platform, his latest clarion call.
So whenever I'm weary, on my last legs,
My energy reservoir down to the dregs,
I think of David, fifteen years older,
I sit up straight and pull back my shoulders.
Say a short mantra out loud to myself,
"Ah sod it, no point in killing yourself."
Take the day off, rest and lay down your pen,
Come back tomorrow and then, try again.

GOING GREEN

How have you got on with plastic free July?
Scored a hundred? Or whole thing passed you by?
How about using the car, mileage down?
Found it was possible to cycle to town?
Working from home has put life under scrutiny
And not just the kids' home-schooling mutiny.
Lives have shifted, altered for good,
Some habits and behaviours that really should.
Which ones will stick? What should we keep?
What will you commit to? Take the leap?
Re-useable cups and bottles for drinks?
That's just obvious to everyone methinks.
But it still takes an effort and at first feels strange
To ditch convenience and make a change.
8 million tons of plastic will enter our seas
And all of it put there by you's and me's.
Now don't get me wrong, I'm no environment preacher,
I'm just starting my journey; I've got nothing to teach you.
But like everyone else, I have imagination
And can dream of a plastic-free beach vacation.
They say every little helps—you know the starfish tale:
By my small tiny actions, I might save a whale.
But there's one big problem I have to solve,
Figuring out how our work might evolve.
I won't lie, I've missed transatlantic travel,
And without conferences, our business unravelled
Pretty quickly: global facilitation; our income stream;
One pandemic later, we're a cat with no cream!
But no use crying over milk that's spilt,
Just because your pinball machine is shouting, "tilt!"
Don't stop, change the way you play.
So that's what I'm doing here today.
I'm going green, with a big green screen.
We're going to become a hybrid conference machine.
It will never replace getting people together,
But it's a great solution to English weather.

If we can use cameras and gizmos and lights,
We can transport delegates to anywhere we like.
And we can have fun once more, live which is neat.
Not chained to the desk, but up on our feet.
And for the planet, we'll be doing our bit,
For maybe one in five conferences this will fit
Our clients' needs, consuming less, saving cost,
And ultimately helping the Earth, before it's lost
To global warming, carbon emissions and the rest.
I don't know if it will work, but I'm giving it my best!
In any case, there's not much choice, as we've seen.
Have a good weekend everyone, and like me, stay green.

As the challenge of
pivoting our conference
design and facilitation
business continued, we
took our first steps into
greenscreen, chroma
key virtual broadcast.
We rehearsed for our
first live event from a
temporary studio. I also
noticed (after the event)
that it had been 'plastic
free July.' It hadn't been
in our house, but I have
begun to take the whole
green agenda a little
more seriously. I've given
up my car and cycle to
work – before anyone is
too impressed, it's about
350 yards.

TALES OF THE

The news headlines are full of
holidaymakers 'surprised' at
rule changes when they arrive
back from abroad. My poem was
inspired partly by this but also by
sessions on resilience we ran for
our wonderful friend and client,
Betsey Strobl. Based on work by
Diana Coutu and Dr Lucy Hone,
we regularly repeat the mantras of,
"Know bad stuff happens, hold a
strong belief that life is meaningful
and always be ready to improvise."

UNEXPECTED

Some people on the news expressed surprise,
They said they could hardly believe their eyes
When the quarantine rules changed overnight.
Home from Spain? Isolate for a fortnight.
"What? You're kidding?! Didn't see this coming."
With hands over ears and loudly humming,
Deaf to the warnings and blind to the signs,
Now temperature checking in border lines.
Wasn't expecting new rules on travel,
Nor for my comfy life to unravel.
Wasn't expecting our business to stall,
Didn't see the car crash coming at all.
Didn't expect virus, Covid-19,
How can you predict something that's unseen?
If there's only one thing we need to learn,
Know that there's a surprise at every turn.
Sometimes they're good, like a windfall you get;
The outsider romps home that was your bet;
The price of the shirt reduced at the till.
It's unexpected but still a small thrill
When your partner agrees with what you've said,
When they laugh, smile, say yes and nod their head.
In my case that's more a shock than surprise
But makes a change from the rolling of eyes.
Unwelcome surprises, causing great harm;
This time your big bet has cost you the farm.
The first rule of resilience, shit happens,
There's proof everywhere, repeating patterns:
Damage or loss to home and property,
Homelessness, famine, disease, poverty.
You can try sticking your head in the sand
But to be brutal, that will only land
You in more trouble, so instead, look up,
Pay attention, be present, buckle up
For the ride, don't hide or take a chance,
Learn the steps and be part of the dance.
Be a team player, look out for others,
Play your part well, for mothers and brothers,
And think carefully, use your common sense,
Each and every action has consequence.
If ever you think you'll not be affected,
Think twice, always expect the unexpected.

MOVING ON

We've handed in our notice, moving on,
Shifting spaces, we're going, going, gone.
Many thinking the same, both big and small,
Don't need a huge office, maybe none at all.
Monster Towers, our mythical working space
In Spencer Yard, secluded hidden place.
We've loved it here, put down our roots,
Literally planted our own green shoots.
But our unscientific survey said,
"Working 9 to 5 is officially dead."
Dolly doesn't like it, all take no giving,
The old-fashioned way to earn a living.
Working from home has been a big success.
No need for commuting—a lot less stress.
So that's it, goodbye, let's all pack our gear,
And work in silos for the rest of the year.
You just need a laptop, chair and a phone,
That's right, "Fly home buddy, I work alone."
Hang on, just a minute, that won't suit me,
Being on your own is, well it's just, lonely.
I need friends, colleagues I play to the crowd,
I know I'm disruptive and sometimes too loud,
But we have it written, value number one,
It's a rule, when at work, you have to have fun.
Covid-19's forced our business to change,
This new way of working feels so strange.
But we don't have a choice, economics are real,
Adapt, shift, flex and quickly's the deal.
So we're off down the road, to make a new start,
To here: 'Smart co-working with a heart'
1, Mill Street, still under construction,
Boldly imagined social junction
Of people, ideas, and collaboration,
Our new home for creative inspiration.
You need community and it needs you

Like many businesses during lockdown, we closed our offices. We moved into a brand-new collaborative working space, 1 Mill Street in Leamington. At the moment there aren't many people to collaborate with, but it is a fabulous environment and we've loved the short time we've been tenants. We're also constructing our own permanent live stream studio. Oh the times, they are a changing!

To be involved, to refresh, renew.
We stand to gain so much more than we'll lose,
It's a chance to cooperate, options to choose
The way we do business, global, local,
Proud of our values, confidently vocal
About issues that matter, and not shy
To say not just what we do, but why.
All of us are moving, in some way shape and form;
Home and virtual working now the new norm.
No one can honestly say what's expected
But whenever you can, stay connected,
And please come and visit, share a latte
Because inside here, we have a café.

Photo of gulls on 1 Mill Street's roof by Rachel Ghent

VIRTUAL LEADERS

For pretty much every one of our clients, large or small, the leading and managing of virtual teams is top of the learning list. It is also still top of mine, since no one is working from our new collaborative office, except me. To some degree I felt qualified, not just to write the poem, but to facilitate online learning on this topic, as we have had remote colleagues for a long time. Now I've re-read the poem, I'm still unnecessarily pleased with rhyming John Kotter with Harry Potter. Sorry.

This week I'm considering, dearest reader,
The challenges of the virtual leader.
Is it harder to lead teams in person,
Than coach and manage the online version?
I've read books on leadership, and motivation,
I've addressed thousands in my imagination.
Principles remain the same, whether crowd
Or Churchillian speeches via the Cloud.
Here's my pros and cons of leading a virtual team
When that team is, well mostly, unseen.

Sensitivity, empathy, build trust
And send gifts on birthdays, it's a must.
Reward team effort with your gratitude
But also look for signs of 'attitude.'

Video conferencing's not just what's spoken,
Beware the one whose camera is broken.
Set management rhythm, cadence sublime,
Something has to fill up all this spare time.
Solid tech systems, processes that match
And an understanding of 'team speak,' "natch."
Is productivity up or down? Who knows?
Pretend you're measuring, it keeps 'em on their toes.
Don't book too many meetings, Zoom fatigue,
Even with agendas, little is achieved.
No jokes, you're not as funny as you think,
And don't start every meeting with a drink.
Treat strugglers and stars as equals in the game,
Ignore petty disputes, nor seek to blame,
Know your purpose, as every player should,
Everyone should strive to make you look good.
Play your part in team sessions that bond
And tackle people issues, no magic wand
For behavioural change, think John Kotter
Rather than hoping for Harry Potter.

The distributed team is the new norm
And it's down to you how they perform.
Whatever 'leadership style' means to you
The shadow of the leader still holds true.
You must proactively create your team,
Have fun, work, play together on machine.
Build an environment where it's nice to belong,
Cool to hang out, and ok to be wrong.
Where each player will support their neighbour,
Partner, collaborate, and lighten labour.
Be a strong leader that's focused, but kind,
Leading the team with a clear yet open mind.
Disciplined, caring, your team will come to see
That online leadership comes to you naturally.

How do I know this? How so clever?
When I've no qualifications whatsoever.
'Virtual Leadership' is my life's adage,
It's real leadership that's hard to manage.

WINDS OF CHANGE

The main talking point this week was the fact that a key conference and event partner of ours had gone into administration (filed for Chapter 11). Combine that with the fact that it was a very breezy day and I had recently been in contact with very good friends who are circumnavigating the globe in their catamaran — come on, surely you can spot all that from the poem?

The winds of change are blowing 'cross the globe,
I can hear them right outside my door.
Sometimes a Beaufort 2, rustling leaves,
Sometimes, a tornado's roar!
When trade winds set fair, predictable,
We sail the economic ocean with ease.
A classy catamaran, slicing through the foam
Adventuring where we please.
For periods of our monster voyage,
We're surging fully powered.
Easterlies, Westerlies, Roaring Forties;
The prevailing winds are ours
Like Thor Heyerdahl, confident,
On his history-making raft,
Sure of goal and destination,
We are certain of our craft.
We've weathered head winds, tail winds too,
We've chartered unknown waters,
And we've treasured, mostly,
What each new venture taught us.
When storms grew strong, blew us off course,
We've called, "all hands on-deck."
We've battened down the hatches,
Made safe and escaped shipwreck
But as every sailor knows, whilst storms are fierce,
There's one wind they all fear;
The dreaded doldrums, stranded, becalmed,
We've been stuck here all year
Like Coleridge's Ancient Mariner,
A boat on painted ocean,
We need a solid breeze,
To put our ship in motion.
We have the skills to navigate,
There's oceans still to cross
And unlike the poetic sailor,
We bear no albatross.
The wind will come, our fortunes turn,
Our resilience will prevail.
We cannot change the direction of the wind
But we can adjust our sail.

OH MY DARLING QUARANTINE

'm not a happy bunny, in fact I feel quite cross,
I even went on radio to talk about my loss.
Came home last night after work, a great day with the team
Filming dancers, presenters too, all against a green screen,
But knowing that for just one month, I have to stay at home
In quarantine, as a second time, they replace Jo's hip bone.
I've steeled myself, been here before, I know it's pretty tough,
She's not that patient, nor as nurse, am I ever good enough?
But reinforcements are at hand, son Harry's on the way
With his help and diplomacy, we'll surely win the day.
There's one key factor for success, on which we both rely,
Hugs and love from Ziva the dog, the apple of our eye.
Imagine then my awful stress, confirming our worst fears,
We're not allowed the dog at home, no strokes, no silky ears,
No fresh air, no countryside walks, no doe-eyed head on lap,
No curling up on the sofa for our shared weekend nap!

In anticipation of Jo's second hip operation, we had to self-isolate for a month. No big deal thought I; I can handle it. That was, until the doctor said I couldn't go outside at all and so the dog had to go away for a month! I even spoke about it on BBC Radio 5 Live phone in with Rachel Burden. As it turned out, the dog loved her holiday, staying with my colleague Alana and her husband Rob.

"What?!! You must be bloody kidding!" I didn't react well,
"Not have Ziva dog for a month, it's worse than, worse than... hell!"
I've had some time to reflect now, consider priority
And, as Jo pointed out respect doctor's authority.
Phoning the radio station, was actually quite useful,
Rachel Burden, broadcaster, pointed out the crucial
Thing was probably the health of, Joanne my darling wife
Rather than the inconvenience of dog-less month of life.
I'm less cross now, though grumpy still, and ready for the test,
Looking forward to a fully fit Jo, pain free and at her best.
She's preparing for the op, and associated pain
Whilst I sort feelings of guilt and not a little shame.
We all have our troubles to bear, many greater than mine
And it doesn't behove any man, to whinge or moan or whine.
So I'll do my best to focus on Jo rather than me.
And when she's fully recovered, they can start on my shoulder, or knee!

POETIC JUSTICE

My corporate poetry is a lovely bit of fun,
A way to reflect when the working week is done.
Things I've worked on, stuff I've read,
To be honest, whatever pops into my head.
Thirty-five weeks now, down the line,
I've just received an email, from a client, in rhyme.
It's a story about our marketing and sales,
Business we measure in sprats, mackerels and whales.
You know us well enough to know we like a laugh,
It's more serious when revenue's been cut in half.
That does strange things to your confidence—you're not to blame
But you still feel anxiety, frustration, and even shame.
You tread a fine line saying things are good, or bad,
Put a brave face on difficult days, or when you're sad.
Easy to get caught up in your internal chatter
You forget to focus on what really matters.
One thing that hurts—no response to emails posted.
It's a modern phenomenon, being ghosted.
We met Barns in 2016, a speaker at TEDx event,
His talk on ripping up the rule book made a dent.
We stayed in touch, then worked with Time Etc.
On influence, communication, and connecting better-er.
Lovely company, friendly culture, warm,
Reflects the leaders, personal development the norm.
Barns wrote a book:
The Hard Work Myth: How to Achieve More and Work Less Hard,
I pre ordered my copy, perfect, just the card.
He called me up, "Let's do more stuff, work again with the team,
They love what you do, I love what you do, living the dream."

Well ok, not that enthusiastic, but plans were hatched,
Just a case of finding dates that matched.
Then Covid, plans on hold, the trail went cold
But then revived when we survived the downturn, sold!
Then all went quiet, when price discussed, then silence reigned.
Resigned there'd be no online workshop, no one trained.
Then yesterday, out of the blue, we received a mail;
Here's the last two lines of his rhyming tale:

"Sorry for the pause, the delay and the all-round lack of fun
Let's push the big button, get cracking and get these sessions done"

It made my day, it really did, lifted spirits, smiles real-wide,
It helped to confirm what I know deep down inside,
There is value in what we do, our clients care
And relationships are strengthened each time we dare
To try new things, take creative risks, and for today, love this:
That my doubts were assuaged in rhyme, poetic justice

More than anything, this poem marked a feelgood moment. When I
began posting the poems on LinkedIn, I thought they would just be a
different way of marketing the company. When Barnaby Lashbrooke,
Forbes, author and client, confirmed their workshops using poetry, it was
an uplifting moment for me and the PM team – we couldn't stop smiling.
It also confirmed what we already knew, that other organisations had
struggled through the reinvention process like ourselves.

THE TIME THIEF

I wish to report a serious crime
Somebody or something is stealing my time
One moment 8.30, starting the day
Then 4pm, where's it gone? Hard to say
Who is the thief, I'm determined to know?
Time's slipping past fast, I need it to slow
Is it, as some say, procrastination?
Or my chief suspect, administration?
The spreadsheets, reports, the numbers to crunch
Or am I taking too long over lunch?
Fat chance of that when I'm working from home
Perhaps I'm talking too much on the phone?
Where have the minutes from my workday gone?
Why, when I look for spare time is there none?
Workforces used to clock in and clock out
Hours in the working day never in doubt
But now at the lap top station, head bent
It's harder to know how much time you've spent
We can't trust the clocks much to my surprise
There's some software purveyors peddling lies
"Download time, 17 minutes precisely"
Good to know, I'll use this free time wisely
Have a break, make the tea, focus renew
Check how long's left. It's gone up! 22!!
Bold promises of software, time savers
Making life easier, do me a favour
The systems boffins, preaching from pulpits
I suspect they're the ones, the chief culprits
'Breakthrough efficiency' other crass words
The truth is days spent resetting passwords

Calendars online, all our futures planned
Should Outlook be applauded, or email banned?
Meetings meet meetings, top of the hour
Each of us locked in our digital tower
So there's your answer, it's a cyber crime
Systems and processes stealing our time
It's the phone and the laptop never closed
That's where all the stolen precious time goes
We're on the edge of the sucking black hole
Stephen Hawking discovered, god rest his soul
Time's fleeting, warping, we dance to its tune
Less chance of stopping it as catching the moon
The world is online 24/7
Cloud computing, the new seventh heaven
And more to come, robots, quantum, AI
Time and you crushed, both squeezed 'til you're dry
Now insidious crime has been deduced
Horological loss can be reduced
If valued time slips from your possession
Make clawing it right back your obsession
Time is finite, the most precious resource
You need to make very best use of yours
Here's why systems steal time with impunity
'cause we victims, provide opportunity
Cyber security protects data online
You need a new shield, to safeguard your time
Stop measuring your life in bits and bytes
Call a halt to long days and longer nights
When you've lost hours, worked without relief
Turn off your laptop and loudly shout. Stop, thief!

Having set myself a weekly deadline, this was the first time that I had to introduce the poem by saying "Last week's poem this week." It would not be the last. In a way, it was quite a good sign because I was beginning to be busy planning and delivering online work and there was less time on a Friday to write, record and publish the weekly poem. Well, that's what I kept telling myself.

THE NEW NORMAL

The video performance of this poem certainly suggested that after week three of isolation, I was going somewhat stir crazy. This short period I had to endure made me more aware of those who had been in total isolation from the start. Due to health reasons, the wonderful graphic artist responsible for the design of these pages has been in isolation from the very beginning of the pandemic and barring hospital visits, still is. I have no idea how he has coped.

'm in my dining room, picture the scene:
I'm working from home, living the dream
Where once was laughter, guests, wine and coffees
Now the detritus of temporary office
Dirty cups and plates awaiting refills
And the evidence of several tea spills
The gentle hum of cooling laptop fan
Intrusive lens of the latest webcam
I used to facilitate live events
Long time ago, performed in circus tents
Now worldly conference facilitator
Meetings creator, fun instigator
Working the crowd has been my life's purpose
Still is, main ring now the corporate circus
But conferences, events have moved online
Less global travel and more daily grind
Short walk from the kitchen, no duty free
Environmentally sound, but hard to please
Audiences, pinned butterflies on display
Neatly arranged in their cases they stay
In their rows, stuck down like collector's card
Fixed, static, communication is hard
Not their fault, virtual limitation
Video a useful imitation
It can't replicate the live experience
Nor can artificial intelligence
There's no magic bullet, no funny hat
Can change the fact that it's, well, mostly flat
Glimpses of life, on screens, that's what we see
We're only living our lives in 2D
So do me a favour, when next on screen
Whether it's Zoom, Webex, Microsoft Teams
Prove your alive, get up, wave, walk about
When your moment comes, maybe scream and shout
And if I'm hosting your next video call
You have permission, anything at all
That proves you're real, and on screen I'm seeing
A 3D, fully rounded, human being.

Humans feel the need to express themselves
But when the words from our lexicon shelves
Are exhausted, when 'unprecedented'
Is heard so frequently we're tormented.
Then we turn instead to analogy,
It's more illuminating than pathology
Or psychology to your average Brit.
It's not that all of us are twits, nitwits,
But we love a metaphor or simile.
It's visual, understood more easily
If we paint a picture, capture feeling,
In every sense it's more revealing.
Instant imagery from what is read,
You might say we've hit the nail on the head.
Are we really "fighting a Covid war"?
Or is this the laziest metaphor?
Combat? Skirmish? Is it really a fight?
I don't think that battle or conflict are right.
Neither is it defence or attack on goal,
Nor is it really a game of whack-a-mole.

ROLLERCOASTER

This poem doesn't need much context really, it just
expresses the feeling that so many have felt, dealing
with the ups, downs, twists and turns of Covid life.
We know the journey and the sensation, because
it's so familiar, but never have so many people wanted
so much to stop the ride.

The visual depictions of the virus are thrilling,
Multi-coloured spikey balls that are killing
Us in our thousands, but what's the deal
with personal experience, how do we feel?
The emotional metaphor of choice?
"Rollercoaster," is most commonly voiced
To describe the last six months, is it the best?
Let's see, why don't we put it to the test?
First, long slow incline—anticipation
Translated—foreboding of each nation,
Then, in turn, our vehicle crests the summit
Before stomach-wrenching, lurching plummet
Headlong, falling, riders gripping the sides,
Holding their breath and bracing their insides
To lessen the impact of the G-force,
Then uncontrollably speeding the course,
Ups and downs, twists and turns, never veering
From fatal rail, but no one steering
Puts us all upside down, corkscrew swerving,
Fellow riders' rictus grins unnerving.
Music blaring, heavy metal, rock n roll
Confirming your car is out of control.
Plunged into darkness, sudden, no warning,
The mouth of the next cave, open, yawning.
As metaphors go, it's pretty good, yes?
It's summed up my journey, more or less.
But the rollercoaster idiom only goes so far,
There's a difference between life and theme park.
On park ride, end is sure, one final drop
Whether thrill or nightmare, it's going to stop,
Pulling into station, restraints release,
You step out, delighted, relieved, pleased.
Not on this ride, no stopping, front or back
Because they're still building, constructing the track!
So buckle-up, hold tight, we're far from done,
This emotional rollercoaster
has plenty more to come.

COFFEE DEMOCRACY

I watched the debate between Trump and Biden
Insightful? Measured? Horizons widened?
No, more a slanging haranguing match,
A political scrap, words bite and scratch.
Millions tuning in, but not listening,
Two old men in combat, ego's bristling.
TV viewers seek confirmation bias,
Each convinced the other side are liars,
Trading insults. He said this, he said that,
He's a fool, he's a softie, playground spat.
"He's killed thousands," "He's killed more!"
He's weak because of the mask he wore.
Moderator, shaping conversation,
Refereeing prize fight for the nation,
The only difference, the colour of their ties.
Men wearing suits peddling tired old lies.
Red side, blue side a permanent fission,
Each argument made driving division.
It's time for 'adversarial' to take a back seat,
"Gladiators' fight!" is democracy's defeat.
Notorious RBG, this statement made,
"Reacting in anger or annoyance will not increase one's ability to persuade."
There's a better way with courage and truth
And remember you can't have truth without Ruth.

The presidential debate, the death of Ruth Bader Ginsburg and a virtual visit to our local TEDx Circle by Ozlem Cekic, were all prompts for this poem. There was no dialogue during the presidential debate – that's for sure – and it was no advert for democracy. Ozlem's story on the other hand is inspiring and one I'd like to focus on in 2021. Do watch her TED talk.

A TED speaker, Muslim MP, a Dane,
Turkish immigrant, Özlem Cekic, her name;
Her inspiring talk I urge you to avail:
'Why I have coffee with people who send me hate mail'
When elected, received death threats, abuse;
She deleted their hate, it served no use.
But a friend advised, reach out to your enemies,
Meet, eat and drink, and dial-up empathy.
No longer distanced political stance
But flesh and blood, handshake, a nervous glance
Meeting haters, abusers, in their home;
One woman with courage visiting alone.
Ten years' worth, she calls it #dialoguecoffee
Personal, responsible, democracy.
If you're shouting at the tv, stop it.
"Don't label people, debate the topic."
That's what Ozlem told us last week on a call
Because we weren't unimportant or too small
To matter, she gave us her time freely
And we discussed, and debated, sincerely.
Don't be part of the silent majority,
Instead be a conduit of diversity.
Choose someone now with opposite philosophy
And invite them round for a tea or a coffee.

was asked to write this week's poem
As my father was overwhelmed at his job.
And so I sat, and I thought, and I lacked... motivation
What topic to set for my own poetic creation?
I could go generic, batter Trump, analyse Biden,
Vent at Boris and Rishi, and those stood beside them.
I could get all depressive, about my own shoulder surgery,
The pain, the medication, the endless seasons of Taskmaster, Mindhunter, MindMaster, Taskhunter,
But this audience is business orientated
And none of my suffering is at all related.
What about Covid? I mean that's old news.
Lockdown in March, October the country is still in review,
Local measures, maybe a Christmas indoors,
Even as I write this, who cares anymore?
Then I got thinking, why is my father so busy?
What does he actually do?
I know it's creative, dynamic and involves groups of people
And the name is something my mates finds unbelievable
But I'm 24, I've known my dad for a fair amount of time
And I still tiptoe around what his profession includes.
Yeah, he uses acting I guess,
He's got a crack team constantly bubbling,
He's passionate about ideas,
Big conference, over Zoom, very impressive.
Purple Monster?
That's vague,
Strange,
Sounds like a theatre company more than what it is
I think,
If I knew what it was,
But I don't.
So what have we learnt?
Not much;
My father is tired
From working, and such,
Perhaps that's enough
Hope this is good enough, and if not, tough...

THOUGHTS IN A SLING

For the second time in the series, my son Harry stepped in as it looked increasingly unlikely I would find the time to write the poem. After his third shoulder dislocation and subsequent operation, he wasn't going anywhere anyway. All the talk was of presidential contests and UK politicians not being up to the job. Pretty much any job.

THE ROAR
OF THE
GREASEPAINT

A funny thing happened to the monsters last week,
We ran a live conference, for Mondelēz Inc.
From the stage of a theatre, a gathered crowd
We presented, we facilitated, we spoke out loud.
There were lights and mics, and prompts in the wings,
There were leaders and speeches and a chance to sing.
A whole heap of technology, blinking away,
Broadcasting, streaming, letting us play
In the way that we love to, engaging first-hand
For a day and half, meticulously planned.
Each attendee taking part from their home
And now appearing again in this week's poem.
All on Teams, we could see people and hear
As if they were right in front of us, crystal clear:
Chef Kwame, Margaret Heffernan, Scott Morrison from Boom,
Dr Natalie Nixon, Ren Washington and artist Devin Liston in the room.
The chat box is great, real time reactions keep you honest.
Enjoying 'amazed,' 'moved,' occasionally 'astonished,'
Time flew by fast, creative output top drawer;
Neither crowd nor monsters wanted it to stop. Encore!
But when the time came to sing our goodbye,
Not ashamed to say there was a tear in my eye.
We work so closely with Sarah, partners and team,
Exploring creativity and collaboration theme.
But like every full on, high energy event,
When it's over you feel totally spent.
I took a few days off, played golf in the rain;
I think about now, I'm ready to start again.
One thing that's different, when virtually at bat,
When the broadcast ends, it feels a little flat.

No hugs, no high fives, no collective relief;
Just silence, screens to black and the strong belief
That it's gone well, logged off attendees are applauding
But no ovations, finishing itself is rewarding.
But oh, how we miss the after-show drinks, the first rosy post-mortem,
The highs, lows, near misses, dropped catches and who caught them,
The roar of the greasepaint, the smell of the crowd,
We do miss them, a bit hollow, a studio bow.
It's been a positive experience, a big success;
It can never replace in-person, but we should do more, not less.
There's no denying environmental gain—
50 States, Canada, UK and not one plane.
The financial comparison? CFO no complaints
And creativity works well in the face of beautiful constraints.
We're going to be like this for a while,
No one is going to be collecting airmiles.
The airways are blocked with Covid-19,
So we'd better stay safe in the space in-between.
Sharing online experiences brings us together
And their final benefit, they work in any weather.

This poem is a celebration of our first full virtual
conference, Collabocon. It was devised in
collaboration with Mondelēz International's North
American marketing team and was a real journey
into the unknown for us all. Delivered to hundreds
of participants across the US and Canada, it was a
bigger success than perhaps any of us dared hope
and more than anything, represented for me the
opportunity to escape from my desk and facilitate
from a large studio. Bliss.

FINANCIAL STATEMENT

This poem is about the serious topic of knowing how your small business is performing. It's important at any time, but seven months into the largest economic slowdown the country has ever experienced, it's even more critical. I do not have a good relationship with spreadsheets, but I am determined to know more. I can happily report that in the first month of 2021, we are still in business. I still can't tell you what our profit margin is, but... one step at a time.

25 years now our business has been going
And throughout that time, numbers have been flowing
In and out of the accounts, amounts that someone
Is carefully monitoring, in theory, but clearly, not me.

This confessional book-keeping entry, states the elementary fact
that, I just don't understand the demands of the spreadsheet.
Dan Bricklin is the man credited with this ubiquitous financial tool.
No fool, he's a Harvard graduate, saving hours of endless calculations.
Finance machinations all Greek to me, but need to be completed, work-sheeted,
neatly seated in cells, columns and rows. Far from the sights and smells
Of the business itself, but capturing and calculating success,
Or revealing another fine mess, you've gotten yourself into.

And now, even luddites like myself
can buy from the shelf accounts packages that, and I quote,
"Give you all you need to run your business, anywhere, anytime."
Well that's just fine, providing the data is correct, but I suspect
It's not always the case. I read some place, that 9 out of 10 spreadsheets
contain mistakes, which makes perfect sense to me. You see, I will often think
we're in the pink when others say we're in the red; will gloomily forecast our last rights,
whilst others are planning celebratory nights. It's not just the accounts, I have similar
trouble with budgets and quotes, it's not just votes that are hard to forecast or count,
the amount of time it takes me to read a balance sheet, woeful.
Margins, P&L, exchange rate fluctuations, debtors, creditors, vexing taxations.
Gross or net, you can bet it will frustrate at a rate I can't calculate.
It's a minefield of maths, with no path that I can see, but others read with ease these
dancing numbers. This week things came to a head as I was led through accrued income and
expenditure, journal entry, plenty to make my head spin, not sinking in but rather drowning me.
They didn't teach finance in my drama classes, or anything that passes for monetary know-how,
but it's no excuse. It's time to smarten up, take fiscal responsibility seriously,
not mysteriously wonder what sorcery it is.
Poetry is all well and good, but I really should know what our profit margin is.

t's been a soggy sort of Halloween,
With notice of lockdown coming between
The pumpkin carvings and spiders' webs,
Sprinkled with a number of notable deaths;
Sean Connery, the original James Bond
Just one of those to pass beyond
The here and now. The birthday, also, All Hallows Eve,
Of my dear departed nephew, Andrew James Neil
Who left this life aged 36, an often-troubled soul
But a human philosopher, who lived life whole
And of whom many stories are constantly re-told,
Bitter-sweet memories we can cherish and hold.
Of chaos and craziness, days and nights wild
Contrast with photos of the golden-haired child.
And it got me to thinking about death,
How we remember those who have taken their last breath.
We've made death bland—western civilization—
The ceremony, celebration, more a sterilization.
We've brushed it under the carpet, rubbed it out,
Made it impolite, an embarrassment and nothing to shout
About. It's enough to say a few words at the crem,
Then file out, look at the flowers and home again.
Cold, unfeeling, a reading maybe a song,

ALL HALLOW'S EVE

Halloween marks the birthday of my late nephew, who
departed this life far too soon, aged 36. Halloween has
become a heavily commercialized 'trick or treat' event
and has lost much of its meaning and relevance, but
contrast this with Dia de Los Muertos, which seems
to me to be a far more respectful way to honour the
departed. It's unsurprising that death is never far away,
when figures are reported on daily news bulletins and
all of the government's diktats and warnings are about
avoiding a deadly virus.

Occasionally celebrants getting the name wrong.
Desperately sad, the loss the grieving, pain
And the aching void knowing you'll never meet again.
Whatever your religion or lack thereof, it's uncertain
What lies beyond the funereal curtain.
But when it comes to remembering the dead,
Surely the Mexicans are streets ahead
With their holiday festival, Dia de Los Muertos.
Something I've only read about and came across
Watching the film Coco,
Singing along with Un Poco Loco,
And learning how they honour, love and respect the deceased;
Dancing, singing, eating and drinking at the very least.
And for some poetic Calaveras and Catrina make-up
And bright beds of marigolds; imagine how that might shake-up
The start of November in England, granted we don't have the weather
To sit outdoors at the cemetery, catching pneumonia not clever,
But we could do so much more to celebrate the lamented, the late.
The dearly departed, for in the end, it is all our fate.
And I'd like to think that a glass might be raised once a year
And that laughter and singing might accompany a tear,
As my memory and spirit is welcomed back home
And that I know for eternity, that I'm not alone.

Biden, Trump, Trump or Biden
Leads that narrow, gaps that widen
A two-horse race, keenly contested
In which half the world is invested
But is it fair, is the race fixed?
Opinions are divided, very mixed
There was no false start at any rate
Both runners were loaded in the gate
Neither are young, both wearing blinkers
And clearly from stables of different thinkers
And they're off, down the straight, around the bend
It's a flat fast race, from beginning to end
Huge excitement in the gathered crowd
Waving flags and shouting out loud
For their favourite, booing the opposition
Cheering as the runners jostle for position
So much at stake, the hopes of a nation
Not to mention personal reputation
Will records be broken in the race this time?
It's neck and neck as they approach the line
What a finish, they've both passed the post
Up to the photo, who's won? who's toast?
But wait, the finish has been extended
It seems the race might not have ended
One rider claims he was pushed on the rail
He's on the track shouting, something about mail
Says there's been cheating, lying and fraud
He says the method of measuring is flawed
He's called for the judges, says he won't yield
Not accepting second place in the field
He's blaming officials, rules, whatever he can
Blaming everything except the way he ran
But despite protestations and claims all fiery
The result will stand, after steward's enquiry
It's hard to lose, when winning is hard-wired
And you can't get your way, with a simple 'You're fired!'

A TWO HORSE RACE

The US presidential election took place on November 3rd, so in theory, I was ready to write this poem about the winner, but as we know, it wasn't straightforward. The drama of President Trump refusing to concede was in its infancy. If you watch the recording, you can see I deliver the words 'You're fired!' with great glee, but little did I know what was to follow. Seems to be a theme that.

WINTER LIGHT

A quick comparison of daylight hours in the UK, between November and July and you can understand why I was yearning for light! If you add our climate to the picture, mostly grey and damp, you can be without sunlight for long periods. Mind you, I did research daylight hours in Tromso, a very northerly point in Norway, and on the same date, they had just 4 hours of daylight. We're lucky!

Christmas is coming, the goose is looking rough;
For me the holidays can't get here fast enough.
We need things to look forward to on such dark winter nights,
So this week I bring you poetry… with lights.
Diwali is coming, in fact I think it's here,
I've seen and heard the fireworks, when the night's been clear.
The lights are up and bulbs are strung across our town,
Each string is primed for its chasing up and down.
Hanukkah is coming, but that's still someway off,
You'll have to wait until the day to say your Mazel Tov.
This Jewish celebration also focuses on light,
Candles will burn in the Menorah at night;
All across the world regardless of belief
Light symbolizes hope—from darkness, relief.
It's no surprise that during winter's rage
We turn to festivals of light, our sadness to assuage.
We fill the sky with dancing lights, lasers onto clouds
And Son et Lumiere shows to wow the crowds;
From Rekyavik to Vegas, Barcelona to Japan
We banish dark with light-shows when and where we can.
We light up pyramids and fountains, buildings old and grand,
We light our bicycles and trams and have light sticks in our hand.
We set the lights to music, classical and pop,
We stand round giant bonfires we never want to stop.
We have primeval urge, to turn towards the glow,
Since during winter the hours of our fiery orb stays low.
When sun appears with weak and watery hue,
The daytime sky remains resolutely pale blue.
We stand with eyes closed, seeking faintest shine,
Even slightest warmth on cheeks and nose feels sublime.
Yet in the darkest times, when we feel we just can't cope,
There's one other way of bringing light, it's sharing hope.
A friendly word, a kindly deed, a simple, "you ok?"
Can help us make it through the night into the light of day.

President Trump's stubborn refusal to accept defeat is the main talking point and at every opportunity, he is tweeting or speaking about a 'stolen' election. It wasn't just Trump either who didn't know when to go. The poem was also pointed at special adviser Dominic Cummings who had resisted pressure for a long time to be on his way. He demonstrated, as many before him, that rules were for ordinary folk and not special individuals like himself. As I write these notes, both men are gone. I personally hope neither ever return to public office.

When they call 'time!' in the pub or when the lights come on in the club;
It's time to go.
When you start to believe your own press and everyone around you is saying yes;
It's time to go.
When everyday a conscious choice is loving the sound of your own voice;
It's time to go.
When you mistake stubbornness for resilience, arrogance for brilliance;
It's time to go.
When you think you're above the law, when 'sorry' sticks in your craw;
It's time to go.
When you've dominated narrative too long, and you're confusing bullying with strong;
It's time to go.
When you label all opposing views with the moniker: fake news;
It's time to go.
If all the people that you hired now make up a list of all that's fired;
It's time to go.
When most of the country are counting the cost of the election you just lost;
It's time to go.
When you're no longer man but mouse and when you're hiding in your house;
It's time to go.
Don't be tardy, don't be slow, don't overstay your welcome, go!
It's time to go!
There'll come a time, like any average Joe, when you simply can't say no
When the finger of fate is beckoning, time to face the final reckoning;
Oh, then you'll know!
It's time to go!

TIME TO GO

GIVING THANKS

It's Thanksgiving weekend in the US and the pandemic has shown there are many kind, thoughtful and generous people; the chance to say thanks is important. In the UK we had a 'clap for carers' each Thursday for a while as a way of thanking front-line health workers, but it became politicised and was halted. Not even giving thanks is straightforward.

Sarah Josepha Hale née Buell
Is not a character that I know well.
When I searched Thanksgiving, up she came
Google, Wikipedia: both have her name
As the person chiefly responsible for this US date.
Celebrated annually across every state,
She wrote letters to the president for 40 years
Advocating a public holiday. Sarah Josepha Hale. Cheers.

It's a simple idea, saying thank you for things,
A bit like I used to, as a child, with harvest hymns,
But more broadly too, taking time across a nation
To consider who and what deserves appreciation.
If ever there was a time, such a moment was needed,
It's right now and perhaps the sentiment will be heeded.
Not just by our American friends but around the globe
As we pause, reflect, give thanks for our blessings and hope,
That there will be better times ahead with fun aplenty
Because let's face it, we've had enough of 2020!

Online this week, with a group of finance leaders
We asked them who they'd like to thank, needless
To say, the list was long, not too many surprises
With partners and family winning the biggest prizes.
They thanked parents and children, husbands and wives
For providing the support to make their working lives
Function from home. They thanked their colleagues for their labours,
They thanked their friends, and one or two, their neighbours
For patience, helpfulness, sometimes beer and wine,
They thanked them all for being generous with their time,
For humour, empathy, for food upon their plate,
For their understanding when they were working late.
The session was fun, great connection, lots of laughs
And a helpful reminder to thank our better halves.
So thank you to the lovely Julia, for helping earn our living
And to all our American friends and colleagues, Happy Thanksgiving.

t's the time of year to write that letter, to put inside the Christmas card
The one that tells family and friends if the year's been easy or hard
It's often filled with tales of adventure, achievements, derring-do
This year it's mostly a list of who's where, what's what and who's who
We began the year in good spirits, January, expectations high
New strategy planned, events fully booked, business success was nigh
There were two slight niggles for the monsters, first Britain entered Brexit
Second, Danielle, our Managing Director, headed for the exit
But a February gig in Arizona, warmed the cockles of our hearts
Great reviews and a short mountain break, gave the year the best of starts
Who could have foreseen, when March arrived, that a virus would go viral?
And plunge our business and a thousand others, into a downward spiral
Shock, anger, denial, bargaining, emotions reeled at the loss
We amongst many, recognized every stage of Kubler-Ross
But knowing that grief curve was helpful, and other models too
And with clients and partners supporting, we began to muddle through
Creativity is our watchword; we gave our imagination some room
We adapted, pivoted, went full virtual, began living lives on Zoom
We adjusted like everyone else to working from home
Connecting daily on video to make sure no one was alone
We were working things out, slowly feeling our way
Made it through April then along came May

A CHRISTMAS
LETTER

The world would reverberate with the name George Floyd
And witness in graphic detail a tragic death, simple to avoid
It is my dearest wish that from that moment on, the world will never be the same
Black Lives Matter and I for one, will continue to say his name
Summer made the lockdowns bearable, six people could meet outside
But some folk were having parties for hundreds, nor trying to hide
Governments around the world, have adopted a different approach
UK, US haven't fared well, Taiwan, New Zealand are beyond reproach
Families, businesses, so many communities have been blighted
But the best outcomes in every case are when people are united
We seemed to favour three-word slogans. Very catchy: Hands. Face. Space.
But when leaders themselves don't stick to the rules, behaviours are all over the place
Talking of leaders, some came and went, though when, it's still not that clear
There might be room in the Whitehouse for two, but I don't think that's the general idea
Lockdowns, tiers, anxiety and fears, masked protests like zombie attack scenes
But there is hope, real scientific hope, with the development of life-saving vaccines
Our business is back on its feet, no travelling for now, safe, protected
But we're taking pride in our on-screen events, we're keeping people connected
And as for next year, well who knows, we'll not predict, we know better
But I'd like to think there'll be more positive news when I get to write the next letter
As for the poems, just a few to go and in the New Year we'll publish a book
52 Weeks in verse, with all money raised going to a cancer charity; please, do take a look.

The thing that distinguishes this poem from all the others in the anthology, is that it's the longest
– isn't that always the case with Christmas letters? It was also late. I've never actually written a Christmas
letter to friends and family and probably never will, but I do confess that I like to read them.

MOTIVACATION

Oh look, it's me, I'm back again,
The next of kin, need a poem, him.
I've been enlisted to help
And I don't half mind
As I've actually got a topic this time.
Motivation, in 2020 the bane of my life,
Endless struggle, constant strife.
Finding small bursts of energy, then long, boring lulls
So many ideas I've started then... oh...
I give up, out of fear, out of anger,
Frustration, boredom, a bit of self-slander.
I find I'm creating endless excuses
To hamper my progress, all equally useless!
The government's shocking, all over the world,
The wage gap, The tax breaks, the social media curse,
There's a pandemic, I'll just wait till it's over;
It's been nine months now, the world's longest hangover...
My arm's in a sling, I'm annoyed and in pain,
I can't focus my mind, again and again.
I'm more creative with reasons for not putting in work
Than with knuckling down, trying, rubbish, useless jerk!
I fantasise next year will be different,
Without doing much to change my predicament
And then, suddenly, late in the year
I alter my path,

I switch my trajectory,
I stop, and notice what needs to change,
I reach out to my mates, they are hugely supportive;
Some with similar struggles that have gone unreported.
I put myself out there, for various roles;
I get recalls, and Zoom chats, from being more bold;
I lay my days out, I compartmentalise.
It's simple, I take one day at a time;
I write simple sketches, but right to the end,
Not stopping in the middle to watch Netflix again.
I exercise, and stretch, and play music, and games;
I make videos, and walk dogs, there's no stopping this train,
And it wasn't some giant epiphany
Or life changing event,
I just made tiny steps, with a small goal in mind.
I wasn't dreaming too big, or wasting my time,
I just made my days busy
With challenges and change
Using my brain, for my mental gain.
There's my lesson, end of session,
Little victories, whatever profession—
Right I'm done.
Hope that helped in some way
Whilst my dad was 'working' or something.

I love this poem. For the third and final time I turned to my son Harry to write the weekly verse, because I was caught up in some end of year virtual events. What I love is that Harry took the opportunity to share his mental challenges honestly as well as poetically, and it was a timely reminder to me about how I might make some changes to my life. I suspect, as no doubt he does, that his poem did more for us both than the last 10 'motivational' Dad talks put together. Not going to stop me doing the next one though.

A LETTER TO SANTA INC.

Dear Santa,
You are clearly a big success
So I'm seeking some advice
I've made a list of things to ask
And I'm going to check it, twice
Your business is so impressive
Your CX is second to none
And your supply chain management
Frankly, outstrips Amazon
Sure, there's a problem with returns
You're not too keen to take things back
Also, not all of the orders
Seem to make it into your sack
But by and large, you get it right
And your reach is truly global
Personalised gifts, wrapped with love
How do you do global yet local?
But there are things that concern me
So I thought I'd ask some questions
About how you run operations
And perhaps make some suggestions
Just one distribution centre
Must make for very crowded shelves
And awkward working conditions
For your exclusive workforce of elves
Diversity is the watchword
For every modern enterprise
So I encourage you to recruit
From every creed, colour and size
The business location is odd

It's acknowledged on the whole
That a hub should sit at the centre
Of your market, not the North Pole!
Hard to see how you make this work
And talking of things hard to see
I'd like to know more detail
Of how you work, financially
Transparency is the key
To being trusted by consumers
Yet no auditor has seen your books
And there are, well, other rumours
For example: this thing about reindeer
And a sleigh that's shipping your freight
Millions of parcels delivered
On time, and on the same date
Your systems must be state of the art
Envied for process, IT
A dream for every CIO
Beyond even… SAP
Yet despite this digital nous
And your enviable brand success
I'm afraid to say, there's a glitch
Your succession planning's a mess
You've done a great job until now
But the modern stresses and strains
Mean you should properly plan
For the next generation to take the reins
You're not in the Fortune 500
But the general rule of thumb
Is to ensure that your board is
50% women in '21
Mrs Claus is fleetingly seen
Depicted mostly at home
But it's clear to any business owner
She's the power behind the throne
So don't hesitate, act right now
Before the next growth of your whiskers
Make Mrs Claus the CEO
And have a Merry Christmas.

I was giving voice to what many were thinking on New Year's Eve. A strong goodbye and get lost to 2020 and a hopeful welcome to whatever '21 has in store. The 'clown' of the story is PM Boris Johnson and the Commedia reference, is Pantalone – he represented high status and money. I'll leave that there. For anyone who has read this far, you might be interested in watching my TEDx talk from 2016, where I argue for the return of the licensed fool.

2020, the year of the poet.
Well for my readers at least and so it
Falls to me to sum it up, to conclude
How badly behaved it's been and how rude.
It's made a lot of people swear and curse,
It's straight up ruined people's lives and worse!
It brought back sweatpants, banned hairbrush and comb
And sent millions to work at home, alone.
For others it meant home-schooling as well;
The impact of that? Too early to tell.
Tested scientific community,
Many bleated 'bout herd immunity.
Some leaders stepped-up, others looked confused
But daily briefings kept us all amused.
The sound advice from Christopher Witty
Juxtaposed with UK's Walter Mitty,
Boris Johnson. Intellect or buffoon?
Archetypal Commedia Pantaloon.
'Cross the pond, election never ending,
Biden's in, but Trump has lawsuits pending.
Darkest hour from Minneapolis came,
P'liceman's knee on neck, George Floyd, say his name.
Hope though, that racism can be shattered
When everyone shows that Black Lives Matter.
So as the year now stumbles to a close,
Most of the talk is when we'll get the dose—
Vaccination from Oxford or Pfizer?
But sadly the stories and the lies are

Already taking hold, doing the rounds,
The news and social media's sights and sounds—
Only thing faster than a pandemic
And there's no cure there. No clever medic
Can help us escape truth's morbidity
To distinguish sense from stupidity.
Conspiracy theories, like viruses, teem;
Some say vaccines aren't always what they seem.
What is certain? On what can we rely?
The year is ending, that we can't deny;
We're in tiered lockdown, no dancing in streets,
You'll have to wait for longer, friends to meet.
We feel hard done to in this worst of years,
Yet, remember parties often end in tiers.
Stay safe, stay home, hold what you cherish near
To 2021, Happy New Year.

THE TIERS OF A CLOWN

ESCAPE ROOM 21

"Come in…" she said, "…welcome to your year ahead.
"This game is new, no one's been here before.
"You think 2020 was challenging,
"This room has the same and then some more.

"Notice your feelings, are you nervous, scared?
"Well that's just fine because the stakes are sky high
"Family, colleagues, friends, your future depends
"on your performance. Come now, don't cry."

I took a moment, to gather my thoughts,
You know, prepare, mentally achieve some Zen.
Picked up a snack, a drink, a magazine
Entitled Procrastination. And then,

She returned, smiling, with a knowing look
handing me a book, on improvisation.
The tour continued. "In this set of drawers,
all of them yours…" oh, the anticipation,

"…are fears, worries, hopes and failures
"to take or leave behind, as you see fit.
"Hanging on the coat-hooks, as you can see,
"Are several ropes and chains, a special kit

"to hold you back, hamper progress, weigh you down.
"You made them yourself, as you're aware.
"But for balance, here are your core values
"and beliefs, which you're proud of, you do care."
Then her eyes narrowed, and in the background
A countdown began. Her voice urgent now, tense.
"When the bell sounds, your challenge will begin
"I'll let you in, to choose your path, make sense?"

I was about to ask some clever questions
When the music struck a beat.
The lights went out all the doors slammed shut
And the guide said, "Take a seat."

"It's almost time," she said, "Put on your helmet
"and your coat. Pockets are filled to the brim
"with courage, curiosity and a huge dose of luck.
"It's time to take your first step in."

One door swung open, light spilled in the room
I could see a far horizon, a golden place;
I crossed the threshold, boldly, head held high,
Then tripped over——fell flat upon my face!

That's how '21 begins, with a false start.
The guide's laughter ringing loudly in our ears.
But pick yourself up, we've been here before,
I've seen an awful lot of New Years.

We'll find a way through the year that's ahead
This game of escape room live, we'll win
Bring it on, '21, come, do your worst
Let the year's business challenges begin.

Whilst every New Year brings hope of a fresh start and new
perspectives, this one began with a new lockdown and
more stringent rules and regulations to avoid COVID-19.
It hit people hard without question. I have never taken part
in an escape room challenge, but Harry, my son has. It was
during a holiday to Croatia and he was properly scared and
failed to escape. It seemed to be the appropriate metaphor
for the year ahead.

DON'T LOOK DOWN

Fred was 13 years old when in July 2019 he was diagnosed with Acute Lymphoblastic Leukaemia, a cancer of the blood. Sadly, his cancer was so aggressive that it did not respond to treatment. After 9 months of chemotherapy, he died in Great Ormond Street hospital in May 2020, aged 14.

From the day Fred was born he lived at full speed. He wanted to go higher, faster, with extra danger. He hated to sleep, never sat still and could always be found conjuring up elaborate plans with his friends. Life was one long episode of Wacky Races. Fred loved anything with wheels. His shed and hallway overflowed with bikes, scooters and skateboards. He spent months building a soapbox with his friend to launch down a hill at top speed.

The *Don't Look Down Fund* was set up in the hope that more children will get the chance to live the life they deserve.

The publication of *Hindsight is 2020* has been a team effort and I would like to express my sincere thanks to:

My family. Jo, Harry and Georgina for their patience, as each weekend was shortened by poetry deadlines. Specifically, Harry for stepping in as guest contributor three times, Georgina for early help with filming and Jo for making sure that the world didn't stop.

Robin Fritz for being the weekly sounding board, editor, motivator and proof-reader.

Craig Spivey for visually making the words and pictures in the book a thing of beauty and thus a joy forever.

The Purple Monster team for a variety of contributions and their continued understanding at work.

Mike Sedgwick for the occasional, but critical, bit of video editing and advice.

Ben Hunt-Davis for writing the foreword.

Anna Thompson and Danielle Thompson who somehow worked out between them how to get all the recordings on YouTube into a play list and in the right order!

All of the clients and colleagues who inspired poems along the way and took the trouble to watch and share them on LinkedIn.

David Hambling for so carefully and thoughtfully editing the poems. I didn't realize I needed an editor until David began work. He was able to use punctuation I've never heard of.

I'd like to say a big thankyou to Sarah Walden for taking the vague idea of creating and publishing a book and making it happen. If you are reading this in print, then it is because Sarah and Craig, between them, know how it works.

And also, to Dulcie Swanston for recommending Sarah in the first place.

My final thanks goes to Ziva our dog, just for being there whenever you need her.

Ziva 2020

Lightning Source UK Ltd.
Milton Keynes UK
UKHW021821050521
383163UK00007B/190